VOICES IN THE DARK

John Pielmeier

BROADWAY PLAY PUBLISHING INC
New York
www.broadwayplaypub.com

VOICES IN THE DARK
© Copyright 2020 John Pielmeier

All rights reserved. This work is fully protected under the copyright laws of the United States of America. No part of this publication may be photocopied, reproduced, stored in a retrieval system, or transmitted, in any form or by any means, electronic, mechanical, recording, or otherwise, without the prior permission of the publisher. Additional copies of this play are available from the publisher.

Written permission is required for live performance of any sort. This includes readings, cuttings, scenes, and excerpts. For amateur and stock performances, please contact Broadway Play Publishing Inc. For all other rights please contact the author c/o B P P I.

Cover art by Modern Dog

First published by B P P I in May 1999
This edition, revised: August 2020
I S B N: 978-0-88145-747-6

Book design: Marie Donovan
Page make-up: Adobe InDesign
Typeface: Palatino

CHARACTERS & SETTING

in order of vocal appearance:
CALLER #1
LIL
OFFICER PARKER
HACK
SOUND MAN
BILL
CALLER #2
OWEN
RED
BLUE
911 OPERATOR(S)
EGAN
MRS EGAN
OPERATOR
DESK SERGEANT

With pre-recording and vocal doubling, it is possible to do the play with one woman and four men. An additional man and woman will be needed, however, for the pre-recording. See Casting and Program Notes, but only after you've read the play.

The action of the play takes place in a radio sound studio and in a cabin in the Adirondacks over a January weekend.

SCENE BREAKDOWN

ACT ONE, Scene One—Friday, 10:45 PM
Scene Two—Saturday, 3 PM
Scene Three—Saturday, 7 PM
Scene Four—Sunday, 5:15 PM
Scene Five—Sunday, 9 PM

ACT TWO, Scene Six—moments later

Parentheses in the dialogue indicate words and phrases that are to be overlapped by the next speaker. They are a cue for this second speaker to begin speaking, not for the current speaker to stop.

NOTE ON MUSIC

For performance of copyrighted songs, arrangements or recordings referenced in this play, permission of the copyright owner(s) must be obtained. Other songs, arrangements or recordings may be substituted provided permission from the copyright owner(s) of such songs, arrangements or recordings is obtained or songs, arrangements or recordings in the public domain may be substituted.

ACT ONE

Scene One

*(Music. In the dark, we hear a young woman's voice [*CALLER #1*], sobbing, hysterical, over a telephone.)*

CALLER #1: Help. Help me. Oh dear god, won't somebody help me?!

(A single light rises on LIL, *seated before a radio microphone and control panel with a red light lit. She is quite attractive and self-assured. As she speaks, her voice is calm and in control, but there are moments when she is not afraid to show her emotion. This call, in particular, hits home hard.)*

LIL: Joyce? It's Lil. I can help. Let me help you.

*(*CALLER #1 *sobs, trying to gain control.)*

CALLER #1: Oh god.

LIL: What's wrong? Joyce?

CALLER #1: I wanna die.

LIL: Why do you want to die?

CALLER #1: I'm so, so ashamed.

LIL: Of what?

*(*CALLER #1 *sobs.)*

LIL: We're all ashamed of some things we do, Joyce. Everybody (does things that they're…)

CALLER #1: *(Lashing out)* What do you know? You don't know.

LIL: You're right. I don't know. Can you tell me?

(Silence)

LIL: Where are you?

(Silence, but for CALLER #1's *gasping sobs.)*

LIL: Joyce, I want to help you, but I can't, unless (you tell me where...)

CALLER #1: Balcony.

LIL: A balcony. Where's that?

(Only stifled sobs)

LIL: Joyce, I want you to come in off the balcony...

CALLER #1: I can't breathe in there.

LIL: Why not?

CALLER #1: I can smell him.

LIL: Who's him?

(No answer)

LIL: Is he there now?

CALLER #1: No.

LIL: Then there's no need to be afraid of him.

CALLER #1: It's not him, it's my fault.

LIL: What did you do?

CALLER #1: It's all my fault.

LIL: Take a deep breath, Joyce. Say it. One sentence. What did you do?

(Silence. When CALLER #1 *finally speaks, the sentence comes hard.)*

CALLER #1: I let Angie spend the night with him.

LIL: Who's Angie?

ACT ONE

(CALLER #1 *starts crying again.*)

LIL: Is she your daughter?

CALLER #1: Yes.

LIL: Will he hurt her, Joyce?

CALLER #1: Yes.

LIL: Who is he?

(A beat)

CALLER #1: He's my father.

(A beat)

LIL: Okay, I want you to come in off the balcony...

CALLER #1: No.

LIL: I can't stop you from doing what you want to do...

CALLER #1: I wanna die.   LIL: ...but you can stop him from...

CALLER #1: I HAVE TO DIE!!!

LIL: JOYCE, WHEN DID THEY LEAVE?!!!

(Silence. Is it too late?)

CALLER #1: An hour ago.

LIL: So you can still stop him.

CALLER #1: No.

LIL: Why not?

CALLER #1: No one would believe me.

LIL: *(Firm)* I believe you, Joyce. I believe you. I know what fathers can do. *(A beat)* Now I want you to go inside. I want you to leave the balcony and go inside. For Angie's sake. Okay?

(A beat)

CALLER #1: Okay.

LIL: And then I want you to do three things.

CALLER #1: What?

LIL: Are you inside?

CALLER #1: Yes.

LIL: Good, Joyce. Now first, I want you to go to your front door, and I want you to unlock it.

CALLER #1: Why?

LIL: I'll tell you in a moment. Just do it.

(A beat. We hear a deadbolt turn.)

LIL: Done?

CALLER #1: Yes.

LIL: Good. Now do you have any childhood pictures around? Pictures of you.

CALLER #1: I don't like to look at those.

LIL: Just this once. You don't have to look at them again.

(Silence. We can hear CALLER #1 *opening a drawer.)*

CALLER #1: Okay.

LIL: You got one?

CALLER #1: Yes.

LIL: What do you see?

CALLER #1: Me.

LIL: How old's "me"?

CALLER #1: Twelve.

LIL: What do you look like?

CALLER #1: Not very pretty.

LIL: Do you look happy?

CALLER #1: No.

LIL: How old were you, Joyce, when your father started doing things to you?

ACT ONE   11

CALLER #1: Eight.

LIL: How old is Angie?

CALLER #1: Six. *(She begins to cry again.)*

LIL: Joyce, because of what you're doing tonight, Angie won't have to hurt like you. Now I want you...

(We hear a door open, voices.)

CALLER #1: Oh my god, who's there? Someone's in the apartment! Daddy?!

LIL: It's okay, Joyce, those are friends. The operator you spoke to when you first called here I D-ed your phone number and these are people who are going to help you. Now listen—stay on the phone a second—the third thing I want you to do is give them your father's address. You're not that little girl any more. After tonight you won't be that little girl again. Okay?

(A beat)

LIL: Joyce? Are you there?

CALLER #1: Yes.

LIL: Be brave. Have hope.

CALLER #1: Okay.

(A male voice, OFFICER PARKER, *takes over.)*

PARKER: *(V O)* This is Officer Parker. Everything seems to be under control.

LIL: She's okay?

PARKER: *(V O)* She'll be fine.

LIL: Thank you.

*(*LIL *pushes a button on the control panel and* CALLER #1's *line is cut off.)*

LIL: We'll be right back, folks.

(The red light goes off on the control panel, as we hear bumper music and an announcement:)

HACK: *(V O)* This is W T L K, Manhattan's all-talk radio, coming to you throughout the city, around the state, across the nation.

(During the announcement, LIL fights to keep her tears inside. A voice interrupts the announcement, coming over the intercom from an unseen booth:)

SOUND MAN: *(V O)* Lil, Hubby on three.

(LIL pushes a button, emotion in her voice.)

LIL: Hi. I got about thirty seconds. What's up?

BILL: *(V O)* You okay?

LIL: Yeah, I just had a close-to-homer. I'll be fine.

BILL: *(V O)* Just called to tell you I may be getting there a little late. The meeting got pushed a few hours.

LIL: Aw, Bill. Will you be there by dinner?

BILL: *(V O)* There's a two pm flight I should be able to make. I left a message with Owen to have Blue meet me at the airport.

LIL: I can't wait to see you. I miss you, Bill.

BILL: *(V O)* Me too, sweetheart. I, uh...

(Bumper music is heard.)

LIL: Gotta go. See you tomorrow.

BILL: *(V O)* Yeah.

(LIL disconnects. A red light goes on.)

LIL: Hi. Welcome back. A lot of us have been hurt very badly by people we trusted, but violence—whether it's against ourselves or others—isn't the answer. It may be entertaining but it's not going to solve our problems. We survive with reason, reserve, and compassion.

ACT ONE

(She pushes another button.) Hi. Welcome to *Last Resort*. You're on the air.

(Silence)

LIL: Hello? You're on the air.

(The voice that speaks is deep, covered, electronically distorted. It overlaps many of LIL's *lines, as if the caller is simply not listening.)*

CALLER #2: Lil?

LIL: This is Doctor Lil. How can I help you?

CALLER #2: This is Daemon, Lil. You got all the answers?

LIL: Hi, Daemon. Of course I don't have all (the answers.)

CALLER #2: I need answers.

LIL: Answers to what?

CALLER #2: I used to think the mind was a lot like electricity—this wild monster we've learned to control to do good instead of evil...

LIL: Why is that, Daemon?

CALLER #2: ...but this woman I know, she messed it all up.

LIL: Why are you disguising your voice?

CALLER #2: I want to hurt her, I want to do terrible things to her...

LIL: Who?

CALLER #2: ...I want to do such awful things and I've got to find a way to stop. *(He sighs—this is hard for him.)* Oh God. Oh my God.

LIL: Who's this woman you want to hurt?

CALLER #2: You've got to help me, Lil, you've got to help me stop.

LIL: I want to help, but I can't unless...

CALLER #2: I've asked for help before but no one listens...

CALLER #2: ...no one knows what's going on, I've killed animals, I've tortured animals...

LIL: Just tell me where you're calling from. Or give me a place where someone can meet you to talk...

CALLER #2: ...but no one believes me, no one cares, this woman will die and no one cares enough to...

CALLER #2: STOP ME!!! *(Silence. Then he laughs.)* You can help me, Lil. I know you can. Only you can give me the help I need.

(Disconnect. There is only the sound of the dial tone. The light fades on LIL's *numbed face. A phone begins ringing in the dark.)*

Scene Two

(The lights slowly rise on the full stage. The phone continues ringing. We are in a cabin in the Adirondacks, in January. This cabin is a hunter's weekend domicile, but a very wealthy hunter he is. It is large, and though one-roomed it is extremely livable. Up-right is a fully-equipped kitchen with food prep island and top-of-the-line appliances; downstage center is a sunken living room with couch, T V [whose screen we cannot see], D V D player, ottoman, and fireplace; up-left is a bubble-wrap-covered Jacuzzi, surrounded by Thermo-Pane windows. Outside the windows hangs a small set of Woodstock chimes, which occasionally tinkle in the wind. Above it all is a bedroom loft, reached by a steep staircase. The ringing phone has extensions in the loft, by the living room sofa, and in the kitchen. In the latter two the phones are cordless, and in the living room it also serves as an answering-machine. The door to the bathroom is left of

ACT ONE 15

the Jacuzzi area, and a sliding pocket door in the stage right wall leads to a large walk-in closet/pantry off the kitchen, though we see only a corner of this room when the door is open. The front door to the cabin is upstage center, and leads to an enclosed mud-room, before taking us outside. There is a window above the kitchen sink, and another in the stage-right wall, the bottom of which has been cracked open and blocked with wood and insulation so that a thick electric cable can pass from outside the window into the room. This cable leads to a distribution box on the floor. The box has an on-off switch, and out of it are coiled several black cables bound together and ending in quadruple power connectors. Though high-ceilinged, the cabin is dark and can be at times gloomily oppressive. Animal heads abound. Animal hides rug the floor and cover the couch. The place has been designed by a man for men, who as boys loved to sit around the campfire and tell ghost stories. It's three PM. As the phone endlessly rings, the door from the mudroom into the cabin swings wide as OWEN, *mid-twenties, wearing a thin jacket and thick-lensed glasses, stumbles in carrying too many suitcases. He staggers to the phone without putting them down, Chaplinesque in his efforts to balance them all while trying to pick up the phone. The luggage falls as he answers:)*

OWEN: Hello?

(No answer. He speaks again into the phone.)

OWEN: Hello?

*(*OWEN's *speech is slow and occasionally he stutters [this is not indicated in dialogue—where this happens is the actor's choice] and soon it dawns on us that this sweet and trusting man is also mentally challenged. At this moment,* LIL, *bundled against the cold and carrying a shoulder-bag and a sack of groceries and flowers, enters the mudroom.)*

LIL: If it's Bill, tell him I'll be right there.

*(*OWEN *hangs up as* LIL *enters the main room.)*

OWEN: It's no one.

LIL: What?

OWEN: No one said hello back.

LIL: Oh. Well, I do that too sometimes.

OWEN: Do what?

LIL: *(Setting the groceries down in the kitchen)* When it's a wrong number, I just hang up.

OWEN: They didn't hang up.

(Someone carrying another grocery bag has entered the mudroom and now cries out.)

HACK: *(O S)* You wanna give me a hand here?!

LIL: Owen?

OWEN: What?

LIL: Never mind. I'll do it.

OWEN: I'll do it.

LIL: Got it, Hack.

(LIL runs to take a torn grocery bag from fifty-ish HACK. A radio veteran, his cynical attitude belies a soft spot for her and success. His New York energy fills the scene—there's barely a moment to breathe until near scene's end.)

OWEN: I'm here to help.

LIL: I know, sweetheart.

HACK: *(Taking in the cabin)* Oh my God, it's Eddie Bauer's clubhouse.

LIL: Owen, you know what you could do?

HACK: Hemingway isn't dead—he's an interior designer in upstate New York.

LIL: *(To OWEN, pointing to the suitcases)* You could take those up to the bedroom.

OWEN: We call it the "deer blind."

ACT ONE

LIL: The deer blind.

HACK: *(Referring to the animal heads)* Don't tell me Bill shot those.

LIL: *(Taking off her coat)* And butchered them too. In a little shed out back. *(Pointing to one of the heads)* I think that one's his first wife.

OWEN: You want me to take these up to the deer blind?

LIL: Thanks, Owen.

HACK: How much does Bill use this joint?

LIL: Two, three weeks.

HACK: A year?

LIL: Don't ask.

HACK: How often have you been here?

(LIL takes a bottle of vodka—Stolichnaya—from the grocery bag, intending to put it in the freezer. OWEN starts picking up all the suitcases.)

LIL: Just the once. My wilderness adventures begin and end in Central Park.

HACK: *(Seizing the Stoli)* I'll take this. You're not drinking again, are you?

LIL: It's for Bill, not me. Hack, I don't want you boozing with a four-hour drive (ahead of you.)

HACK: I'm not boozing—I'll just have the one. Jeez—I thought *Ruth* was the Vodka Nazi.

LIL: Ruth's on the wagon?

HACK: *(Pouring himself a drink)* Thanks to your angelic example.

OWEN: *(To himself)* I'll do it. I'm here to help.

LIL: Owen…

HACK: I can't believe we needed a physical map to find this place.

LIL: We're in the mountains. The Internet's for shit.

HACK: No cell reception?

LIL: You're better off with two cups and a string.

(OWEN *collapses with the luggage.*)

OWEN: Whoops.

LIL: Owen, sweetie...

OWEN: Yep?

LIL: ...maybe you better take those up one at a time. Okay?

HACK: What happens when you wanna leave the Frontier? How do you call a cab?

LIL: I use the land line. We may not be in the 21st century up here but we're close.

(As OWEN *starts picking up the luggage*)

LIL: Owen? Did you hear what I said?

OWEN: Okay.

HACK: Lil, we gotta talk.

LIL: You had your chance in the car.

HACK: You were asleep.

LIL: I was exhausted. Anyway, the answer's no. Now get outa here. I want to be alone when Bill arrives...

HACK: Don't worry, I won't spoil your little play-date. I just...

LIL: It's not just play.

HACK: Okay, you got a marriage to save. Big deal. Why can't Tarzan move to the Big Apple and let *you* bring down the antelope?

LIL: He's got something called a penis?

ACT ONE

HACK: Oh yeah, I used to have one of those. Now I got a credit card. It's much better. Speaking of penises, where's the bathroom? I hope it's inside.

OWEN: It's in there with the toilet.

HACK: Thank you. *(An aside to* LIL*)* My God, I'm in *Deliverance Two.*

(Drink in hand, HACK *heads to the bathroom as* OWEN *finishes picking up all the suitcases, muttering:)*

OWEN: I'll do it…

LIL: Owen…

OWEN: …I'm here to help.

LIL: …I don't think you can.

OWEN: You don't want me to do just what you think I can do, do you?

LIL: Of course not, I just…

OWEN: Then don't underestimate me, Doctor Lil. No one ever allows me…

LIL: Okay, go to it, Owen—get 'em up there.

OWEN: Cause you know what?

LIL: What?

OWEN: *(With pride)* I got a penis too.

LIL: We all do, Owen. Some just hide it better.

OWEN: I don't got a credit card, though.

LIL: You're a lucky man.

(As OWEN *slowly climbs the stairs with the suitcases,* LIL *proceeds to unpack the groceries, putting everything away in the kitchen or the pantry. Included in her unpacking are several magazines, newspapers, and a local map which she places on the coffee table in the living room, the flowers which she puts in a vase, and a be-ribboned box of cigars for* BILL.*)*

LIL: Has Blue left for the airport?

OWEN: Huh?

LIL: To pick up Bill. You gave him the message, right?

OWEN: Ooops. I forgot.

LIL: Oh god. Owen.

OWEN: I could pick him up. 'Cept I don't got the van.

LIL: No, that's okay.

OWEN: Maybe I could take your friend's car. 'Cept I don't got a license.

LIL: That's okay, Owen.

OWEN: I'll drive real slow.

LIL: Don't worry. Bill will just get a cab.

(A toilet flushes...)

OWEN: *You're* worried, ain't ya?

LIL: I'm anxious. There's a difference.

(...and HACK enters from the bathroom.)

HACK: Now before I slalom out of here...

LIL: I don't want to talk about this.

HACK: ...Fox needs an answer by Monday.

LIL: They have an answer.

HACK: They want a yes.

LIL: They want callers like the guy last night. Did they find him? Did they trace the call?

HACK: Yeah, yeah, it was nothing.

LIL: Nothing?

HACK: They traced it to a house in Pittsburgh—the owners were away in Florida, but listen...

LIL: Who was he?

ACT ONE

HACK: The house-sitter, I guess. Fox heard it, they loved it.

LIL: What did I tell you?

HACK: Primal reality programming. Live.

LIL: Where psychos murder innocent women.

HACK: No one was murdered! You heard him laughing. It was his idea of a sick joke. But because of that call, Fox is increasing their offer.

LIL: Oh my God. Hack, if I didn't know any better, I'd figure you put the guy up to it.

HACK: I would never do a thing like that.

(OWEN *makes the loft with all the luggage.*)

OWEN: I did it!

LIL: Good for you!

HACK: I'll admit it's not a bad idea, but…

LIL: This just proves my point. It doesn't matter to Fox whether he was a killer or a practical joker, what matters is that people tuned in. End of discussion.

HACK: What matters is that phone call went viral in five minutes! No wonder you're the number one radio show (in the country…)

(OWEN *opens a suitcase and takes out clothes.*)

LIL: I'm the number one freak show! I attract these people, Hack. No woman calls me any more because she's mildly irritated with her husband's snoring. She's calls because she wants to cut out his snore-box with a butcher knife!

HACK: And what's the name of the program? *Last Resort.*

LIL: That was your idea, not mine. Owen, what are you doing?

OWEN: I'm unpacking.

LIL: I'll do it.

OWEN: I'll do it.

LIL: I'll do it, Owen.

HACK: This is the twenty-first century, Lily-pad. People are desperate and they need someone who can fix 'em (before things get worse.)

LIL: I don't fix 'em, I point 'em in the right direction. Like I'm doing to you. There's the door.

HACK: You know how many lives you've saved because of your show?

LIL: Seveny-nine.   HACK: Seventy-nine.

HACK: And you don't want to go on national T V? You'd increase that number ten-fold. Seven-hundred-ninety human lives you'd have saved by now.

(OWEN *sticks a pair of her brightly colored socks in his back pocket.*)

LIL: Owen, what are you putting in your pocket?

OWEN: Nothin'.

LIL: Those are my socks. Please put them back.

OWEN: Okay. *(He picks up a can of air freshener and sprays the loft.)*

LIL: I'm a voice, Hack—that's what I do best. I listen to someone in need and I offer simple suggestions. Owen!

OWEN: I'm freshenin'.

LIL: Well stop freshening and come down from there. Okay?

OWEN: Okay.

HACK: Lil, I'm not asking you to do anything different than what you're doing now. It'll be a call-in show! You'll talk to the psychos over the phone.

ACT ONE   23

(LIL *begins to make herself a cranberry and seltzer, searching the cupboards and the refrigerator.*)

LIL: You really think millions of people are gonna sit and watch some boring therapist...

LIL: ... nod sympathetically to a voice on the other end of a phone line?	HACK: You are not boring! Listen to me.

LIL: *(To* OWEN, *coming down the stairs)* Sit. *(To herself)* Where's the goddamn seltzer?

HACK: This is important television, Lil!

LIL: "Important television" is an oxymoron!

OWEN: You want the goddamn seltzer? *(He goes to the closet/pantry, slides open the door, and disappears inside.)*

HACK: Listen to what Fox has in mind.

LIL: Hack, what don't you understand about the word "no"?	HACK: They can trace a call in seconds, right?

HACK: Some desperate person calls you, like that Balcony Lady last night. Fox finds out where she's calling from, they have a local affiliate camera crew on the site within minutes. They got a camera running up to her apartment with the police, breaking through the door, rushing onto the balcony...

(There's a crash of smashing glass from the pantry.)

LIL: What's going on in there?!

OWEN: *(O S)* I'll do it!

HACK: ...they got a second camera with the abusive father. You talk to him, you speak to the little girl, the guy's arrested, the kid's returned to her weeping mother's open arms—you gotta time it to commercial breaks, sure, but things get done!

(OWEN *enters with a bottle of seltzer. The phone rings.*)

HACK: That's the ad campaign—tune in, folks, an hour later Lives Will Be Changed.

OWEN: Found the goddamn seltzer.

LIL: What happened in there?

OWEN: Accident.

(OWEN *gives* LIL *the seltzer, grabs a rag, and re-enters the closet/pantry to mop up as she goes to answer the phone.*)

HACK: The other stations might as well go off the air while your show's on.

LIL: Hello, you're on the air—oh god.

(*An accent from the deep South asks:*)

RED: *(V O)* Hello? Is Margaret there?

LIL: I'm sorry, I thought I was...

RED: *(V O)* Margaret? Is that you?

LIL: You got the wrong number.

(LIL *hangs up as* OWEN *enters from the pantry, with a red rag to rinse.*)

HACK: Are you saying "no" because of Bill?

LIL: I'm saying "no" because— (*Alarmed, to* OWEN) Oh my God—are you bleeding?

OWEN: I broke the pickle beets. Looks like blood, but it isn't. (*He exits to the pantry with a clean rag.*)

HACK: You're turning down an umpteen-million dollar deal because your husband doesn't have the balls to let you be the man of the family!

(*The phone rings.*)

LIL: It's not just Bill. I've been thinking about this for a long time. (*Answering the phone*) Hello?

RED: *(V O)* Margaret? Is that you?

ACT ONE 25

LIL: You got the wrong number! *(She hangs up.)* Hack, I'm not only not doing the T V show, I'm stopping the radio broadcast too. *(Silence, for the first time in the scene.)* I want to deal with people in the *middle* of their rope, not at the end of it.

HACK: You gotta be kiddin' me.

LIL: I've made up my mind. I'm moving back to D C…

HACK: Lil…

LIL: …Bill and I are resuming a normal life…

HACK: What about me?! What am I gonna do, Lil?! *(A beat)* I've been working thirty-two years in this business and this Fox deal is the only thing standing between me and a retirement trailer in Altoona, Florida!

LIL: Oh, come on, Hack…

HACK: *(Pointing to a deer trophy)* You might as well cut off my head and hang it next to Bambi up there, cause I'll level with you, Lily-Pad, I am broke! I'm too old to start over, I'm way behind on my tax payments…

| LIL: Don't hold me responsible for your financial… | HACK: …the I R S is breathing down my neck… |

HACK: GODDAMMIT, DO NOT DO THIS TO ME!

(The phone rings again. LIL*'s right on it.)*

LIL: Check your number! There is no Margaret here!

(Instead of RED, *we hear the distorted voice of* CALLER #2.*)*

CALLER #2: Hi, Lil. It's Daemon. Remember me?

(Silence. LIL *freezes.)*

LIL: What do you want? How'd you get this number?

*(*OWEN *enters again, heading for the sink.)*

CALLER #2: I need your help, Lil. I want your help. Only you can give me the help I need.

(CALLER #2 *laughs*. OWEN *washes up*.)

OWEN: Looks like blood. All over.

(Fade to black. Music)

Scene Three

(As the music ends, thunder rumbles and the lights rise on LIL, sitting on the couch with a non-alcoholic drink in her hand and reading a book. She's lit by a reading lamp and firelight from the fireplace. It's seven pm. The rest of the room is dark. Outside, a thunderstorm drops light snow. Throughout the scene, the storm gets closer. Lightning occasionally illuminates the woods outside the cabin, though at first not at the same time as we hear the rumbles of thunder. As the scene progresses, the lightning and thunder come closer together, and the thunder gets louder. We occasionally hear the tinkle of the Woodstock chimes outside the Jacuzzi windows. After a moment the phone rings. She makes no move to answer it. The answering machine picks up after the second ring.)

BILL: *(V O. Recorded)* Hi. If you know I'm here, leave a message. Otherwise, call me in D C.

(After the beep, BILL's voice, live this time, calls out:)

BILL: *(V O)* Lil? You there?

(LIL picks up the phone, relieved.)

LIL: Hi.

BILL: *(V O)* Hi. How's everything?

LIL: Where are you?

BILL: *(V O)* How was the drive?

LIL: Fine.

ACT ONE

BILL: *(V O)* Place okay?

LIL: Yeah, if you like dead and furry.

(BILL *laughs.*)

LIL: Where are you? Did you miss your plane? I tried to call...

BILL: *(V O)* They cancelled it.

LIL: You're kidding.

BILL: *(V O)* Nope.

LIL: Why didn't you call earlier? I tried your cell but you didn't pick up.

BILL: *(V O)* I've been on the phone all afternoon. Things have been crazy at work...

LIL: *(Firm)* Why aren't you here, Bill?

(A beat)

BILL: *(V O)* I'll be there before you know it.

LIL: I want you here now.

BILL: *(V O)* Is something wrong?

LIL: Yeah, some practical joker phoned the show last night. He distorted his voice—it freaked me out. And then when I signed off I said I'd be broadcasting from here next week and no sooner do I walk in the door when he calls again. How'd he get hold of this number? I didn't know you were even listed.

BILL: *(V O)* He's threatening you?

LIL: He says he wants my help.

BILL: *(V O)* Like who doesn't? Have it traced.

LIL: They did that. He's calling from Pittsburgh, hundreds of miles away. After he called here Hack phoned the local police but they said they couldn't (do a thing...)

BILL: *(V O)* Is Hack still there?

LIL: He's meeting Ruth in Vermont for the weekend. I thought you'd be here any minute so I told him to leave. When are you getting here?

BILL: *(V O)* There was a bomb.

LIL: What?

BILL: *(V O)* Somebody called in with a bomb threat. That's why the flight was cancelled.

LIL: You're kidding.

BILL: *(V O)* And there's not another connecting flight up there til Monday.

(Silence. Thunder)

BILL: *(V O)* I could take the train. Want me to take the train?

LIL: Why didn't you call me?	BILL: *(V O)* I wouldn't get in til late tomorrow night but (if that's what you want...)

LIL: Why didn't you call me sooner?

BILL: *(V O)* Something came up, some bullshit. Look, if you need anything...

LIL: What bullshit?

BILL: *(V O)* Work bullshit. The negotiations hit a snag, so when the plane was cancelled I went back to the office (to straighten things out...)

LIL: You mean you totally forgot about calling me?

BILL: *(V O)* Look, sweetheart, don't make a big deal out of this...

LIL: It *is* a big deal.

BILL: *(V O)* They cancelled the flight, I went back to the meeting...

ACT ONE

LIL: I'm talking priorities here...

BILL: *(V O)* I *meant* to call but...

BILL: *(V O)* ...I had problems to fix.

LIL: We have a marriage to fix.

LIL: And you don't even have the decency to let me know you'll be late?!

BILL: *(V O)* I'll be on the next plane. I'll be there Monday, for crying out loud!

(Thunder. BILL sighs, still pissed.)

BILL: *(V O)* I'm sorry, okay? I'll check in with you tomorrow, I promise. If that joker bugs you again, don't hesitate to call. Call my cell, not home. The meeting's at a client's apartment—we'll be here til midnight.

LIL: What client?

(A beat)

BILL: *(V O)* Someone (you don't know...)

LIL: Are you at Jane's?

BILL: *(V O)* No.

LIL: Don't lie to me, Bill. I can check this out.

BILL: *(V O)* I'm not lying.

LIL: "Something came up." Did Jane come up?

BILL: *(V O)* It's business, sweetheart, I give you my word...

LIL: Is she the reason you didn't call me right away?

BILL: *(V O)* Jane's history, she's fired...

LIL: Is she the reason you're staying these extra two days?

BILL: *(V O)* ...she's out of my life!

BILL: *(V O)* Everyone feels that if I'd gone up there (without settling...)

LIL: I don't care what "everyone feels", I want to know what *you* feel.

BILL: *(V O)* Can you please stop being my therapist (for five fucking minutes…)

LIL: Can you please stop avoiding (my question?)

BILL: *(V O)* I am not your goddamn patient!

LIL: *(Exploding)* Then fuck you, you stupid shit! How's that for a non-therapeutic response?!

(LIL *hangs up. Thunder. The phone rings. She picks it up and slams the receiver back down. She takes the flowers and dumps them in the trash, then goes to refill her drink. On the spur of the moment, she opens the freezer and takes out the vodka. She fills her glass and returns the bottle to the freezer. She pauses before drinking, then pours the drink into the sink. She looks at the glass, wets her finger with what's left of the contents, and licks it. Silence. Fighting emotion, she wanders down to the D V D player, wondering if the phone will ring again. Noticing a stack of D V Ds, she picks them up and reads the titles, laughing in spite of herself:)*

LIL: "Romancing the Bone." "Forrest Hump." Oh, Bill.

(Thunder. The phone rings. LIL *answers the phone.)*

LIL: Guess what I just found, you horny bastard?

RED: *(V O)* Margaret? Is that you?

LIL: *(Embarrassed laughter)* Oh God. No.

RED: *(V O)* I guess I have the wrong number again.

LIL: I guess you do. Who's Margaret?

RED: *(V O)* My girlfriend.

LIL: Well, she couldn't be much of a girlfriend if you don't know her phone number. Good night.

(LIL *hangs up, then returns the D V Ds to their place. The phone rings.)*

ACT ONE 31

BILL: *(V O. Recorded)* Hi. If you know I'm here, leave a message. Otherwise, call me in D C.

RED: *(V O)* Do you have any idea where Margaret *is*?

(LIL *laughs and picks up the phone.*)

LIL: No I don't. But let me give you some advice. What's your name?

RED: *(V O)* Red.

LIL: Red, you need to find yourself another girlfriend.

RED: *(V O)* Are you available?

LIL: *(Laughing)* No.

RED: *(V O)* Why are you laughing? You did just call me a horny bastard when you picked up. Who'd you think I was?

(A beat)

LIL: My husband. Good night, Red.

RED: *(V O)* Can I give *you* some advice?

(A beat)

LIL: Sure. Why the hell not?

RED: *(V O)* What's your name?

(A beat. LIL *hesitates, then:)*

LIL: Lil.

RED: *(V O)* You gotta apologize, Lil.

LIL: To my husband?

RED: *(V O)* To *me*!

LIL: Why?

RED: *(V O)* Cause you're not Margaret!

(LIL *laughs at that.*)

RED: *(V O)* I mean I'm sitting here in a motel room in Plattsburgh, New York, never been this far north in my life…

LIL: You sound like it.

RED: *(V O)* …my date stands me up, *you* let me down…

LIL: How did I let you down?!

RED: *(V O)* You're married. To a horny bastard!

(LIL *laughs.*)

RED: *(V O)* At least I got you laughing. Why'd you call him that? Did you two have a fight?

LIL: If you're trying to pick me up, it won't work.

RED: *(V O)* I'm not trying to pick you up! I'm asking as a concerned human being. If you and your husband are fighting, I wanna help you out.

LIL: Are you a qualified therapist, Red?

RED: *(V O)* Hell, yeah.

(LIL *laughs.*)

RED: *(V O)* So tell me. What's your problem?

LIL: You're very sweet but I'm not going there. Goodbye.

(LIL *hangs up. After a moment the phone rings again. She picks up.*)

LIL: Please don't call any more, Red.

RED: *(V O)* Do you love him? Do you still love him?

(A beat. Thunder)

LIL: Yes I do.

RED: *(V O)* That's good. Is he funny? Does he make you laugh? Especially in bed. That's more important than anything, in my opinion. Hey, I take off my clothes,

ACT ONE

women are rollin' in the aisles. Talk about stand-up comedy.

(Laughing, LIL sits on the edge of the Jacuzzi, her back to the windows. Lightning illuminates the empty window behind her. Then:)

LIL: He makes me laugh in lots of ways, Red. I couldn't live without him. Now you have a good night.

(Deafening thunder, as lightning illuminates a dark silhouette—someone bundled in a large hooded parka—standing outside the Jacuzzi window behind her. She is completely unaware of this presence. But she is startled by the thunder.)

LIL: Jesus.

RED: *(V O)* I know where you're coming from, Lil. I love my kids, I miss my ex—hell, I see her every day. She's on the force, same as me.

LIL: The force?

RED: *(V O)* I'm an officer of the law. Chattanooga, Tennessee. Shield number 87923. I'm up here for a police convention.

LIL: You're a cop?

RED: *(V O)* I know, I know, I lose more dates this way.

LIL: Like Margaret?

RED: *(V O. Laughing)* Like Margaret.

(LIL laughs too.)

RED: *(V O)* Listen, you, uh, you wanna meet for a drink?

LIL: No. Good night.

RED: *(V O)* I'm talking drinks, not elopement.

LIL: Thank you, Red. You sound like a lovely guy. But I'm a married woman…

RED: *(V O)* Married to a horny bastard.

LIL: *(Laughing)* I don't even know your real name. Which I'm sure isn't "Red."

RED: *(V O)* It's John Lone Wolf. One-quarter Native-American, three-quarters Scotch-Irish, one hundred percent Southern Baptist.

LIL: *(Laughing)* Now you're really scaring me.

RED: *(V O)* My picture's on page three of the Plattsburgh Press Republican if you want to check me out.

LIL: Really? *(She picks up the paper from the coffee table and opens to page three.)*

RED: *(V O)* Yeah. They got an article on the convention. I'm the keynote speaker.

LIL: *(Spotting his picture)* That's you?

RED: *(V O)* Yours truly. Hey, tell you what—call up the Convention Center and talk to any one of the guys there. They'll tell you I'm exactly who I say I am. Then, if you feel okay about it, we'll get together tomorrow some time. Just drinks and conversation, nothing else. In a very public space.

(Lightning. The figure outside the window is gone. LIL *opens the ribboned cigar box and takes out a cigar.)*

LIL: I don't think so, Red.

RED: *(V O)* Come on! You need this, Lil. In my opinion as a qualified therapist...

LIL: *(Lighting the cigar)* I thought you were a cop.

RED: *(V O)* Cops are just therapists with guns, Lil.

*(*LIL *laughs.)*

RED: *(V O)* Besides, I have a feeling.

LIL: A feeling?

ACT ONE

RED: *(V O)* You're in trouble and I'm gonna bail you out.

(LIL *smiles. Thunder. The storm is receding.)*

LIL: Okay—there is one thing you could do for me.

RED: *(V O)* What's that?

LIL: Some guy's been calling me. Nuisance calls. He's house-sitting in Pittsburgh. Do you think you could ask your cop connections to pay him a visit and make him stop?

RED: *(V O)* Well, I'll do my best. Do you have an address? A phone number?

LIL: No but I can get it in the morning. How can I reach you?

RED: *(V O)* Got a pencil?

LIL: Hold on. *(She looks for a pencil, finds one.)*

RED: *(V O)* It's a direct dial to the room where I'm staying. My cell's for shit up here.

LIL: You're telling me. Okay—ready.

RED: *(V O)* 518 555-6429.

LIL: Thanks. I'll call you first thing tomorrow. I appreciate it.

RED: *(V O)* My pleasure. Does this mean we have a date?

LIL: *(Laughing)* No, it does not. Good night.

RED: *(V O)* Good night.

(LIL *hangs up, smiling. Sighing, dimly lit, she puffs on her cigar. Thunder. Lightning. Fade to black. Music)*

Scene Four

(As the music ends and the lights rise, we discover BLUE, *fifty-something, big, overweight, standing in the middle of the room wearing a hooded parka. He is missing the end of a finger. The food prep island holds a package of veal and a cutting board of fresh vegetables—carrots, celery, parsley—waiting to be sliced, chopped, and dumped in a large stew pot sitting on the stove. From the curtain rod over the kitchen window hangs Lil's clothing for the evening. It's 5:15, and already night is beginning to settle.)*

BLUE: *(Talking to Lil offstage)* ...so the kid is kneeling there, the F B I just left, the C I A is on the way, he knows something or someone is out to get him, right? And he falls down in this big pile of dirty clothes -stockings and girdles and bras, you know?—that have been sitting there for months because his mother was murdered before she could do her laundry? And he falls down in this pile of dirty clothes in total despair, and—are you ready for this? His mother's bra eats him.

(The phone rings.)

BLUE: Want me to get that?!

LIL: *(O S)* It'll pick up!

(After the second ring, the answering machine answers:)

BILL: *(V O. Recorded)* Hi. If you know I'm here, leave a message. Otherwise call me in D C.

(As the message plays, LIL *appears in the pantry doorway, carrying the parts to a Cuisinart or its equivalent. She listens for the caller. After the beep, there is only the sound of the party hanging up.)*

BLUE: Wrong number.

LIL: Yeah. *(She goes to the food prep island and assembles the various parts.)*

BLUE: So what do you think?

ACT ONE

LIL: About what?

BLUE: The bra eating him.

LIL: What do you mean?

BLUE: It's hungry, it's like a cannibalistic bra.

LIL: You mean it has teeth?

BLUE: No, it's just a metaphor, like his mother, you know, is out to get him and her spirit invades her underwear and—aw, screw it, it's just a story.

LIL: I see. *(She plugs it in—)*

BLUE: It's a dumb story. Pretty scary, though, right?

(—but the machine won't start.)

LIL: Damn.

BLUE: You think it can be published?

LIL: I don't know, Blue, I'm not in the publishing field. Do you know what's wrong here?

BLUE: Yeah, you gotta flip that switch. By the plug.

(BLUE *flips on a wall switch beside the outlet.* LIL *tries the machine—)*

BLUE: You'd be surprised how many people make that kind of mistake.

(—it works!)

BLUE: That's one of the first things I learned in my online electrician course—make sure the power's travelin' from the outlet to the machine. Hey, can I give you a hand?

LIL: That's okay, I just—

BLUE: *(Taking off his parka)* Let me give you a hand. We don't got much time 'fore we gotta leave. *(Grabbing the stew pot)* I'll fill this with water, how about that?

LIL: *(Resigning herself)* Sure, why not?

(BLUE *fills the stew pot with water as* LIL *peels carrots.*)

BLUE: See, electricity's like this Frankenstein monster we've taught to do good instead of evil, but you gotta understand it to make it work.

LIL: *(Making conversation)* Are you an electrician?

BLUE: Not officially but I'm really good at it. Like you shoulda seen me Friday with that guy from your show? I coulda told him right off this place didn't have the kinda power he needed.

LIL: What guy?

BLUE: From your show. You needed a bigger electrical feed for the radio broadcasts all next week.

LIL: The guy from New York?

BLUE: Yeah. See this box?

LIL: Hack said he was coming Monday.

(BLUE *crosses to the distribution box and the coil of cable ending in the power lines.*)

BLUE: He was on some kinda schedule, I don't know. We hooked direct up to the transformer outside. Completely bypassed the fuse box.

(Demonstrating, BLUE *flips the switch on, and a bright red light lights on the box.)*

LIL: Did he install more phone lines?

BLUE: *(Flipping the switch off)* No, just power. The phones are comin' later. I mean, I couldn't believe how stupid he was. We lose electricity twenty, thirty times a year here—

(The phone rings again. After two rings it picks up, and we hear BILL's *message.* BLUE *continues talking over it all.)*

BLUE: —these cordless phones go dead. You'd have to use the rotary upstairs (if anything happened—)

ACT ONE

LIL: I can't run the show on a rotary.

BLUE: That's what I told him! "Who's the pro here?" I said. You get a semi in here with a coupla generators you'd be sittin' pretty—

(LIL *shushes* BLUE *so she can hear the caller. After the beep, the caller hangs up.*)

BLUE: Could be the F B I. They harass innocent citizens just for the heck of it. *(Returning to the kitchen)* See, I could be a pro, no problem. I could do what some ass-kissing Union guy does and make a lot more money if I wanted to. I could get hired by some big New York hot-shot company but I made a choice to stay here. *(Enough water?)* How's this?

LIL: Fine. How long have you lived here, Blue?

(BLUE *puts the pot back on the stove.* LIL *puts carrots through the Cuisinart.*)

BLUE: Long time. I mean anyone can write stories, it takes a pro to hook 'em up to the juice. You wanna know my secret? My stories are autobiographical. All the great American writers—Mikey Connelly, Stevie King, Johnny Grisham—I mean, the common reader wouldn't realize it, but someone like you, a Famous Celebrity Psychologist, you read one of their books, you see right into their heart.

LIL: Are your parents still alive?

BLUE: Oh, man, there's a story. You got about six hours? They're drivin' down this road alone one night—

LIL: What time is it?

BLUE: *(Checking his watch)* Ooooh, later than I thought. We gotta leave in about ten minutes.

LIL: Oh God. Would you chop up this onion and put it in a skillet? *(She takes a cast-iron skillet and puts it on the stovetop.)*

BLUE: Sure. Happy to oblige.

LIL: Thanks, Blue. I really appreciate this.

(BLUE grabs a large butcher knife and starts to chop the onion.)

BLUE: I enjoy the company. Not many pretty women to talk to in this neck of the woods. But you, a Famous Celebrity Psychologist, you must have people talkin' to you all the time, revealin' their true inner selves—

(LIL puts the celery through the machine, not watching what she's doing.)

BLUE: Whoa, careful there, you could hurt yourself!

LIL: I'm fine.

BLUE: I wouldn't trust that thing. It's like something out of one of my stories. Machine comes alive, chews your fingers off. Looka this. *(Holding up his half-finger)* Goes to show you, you gotta pay attention to what you're doin'. *(He goes back to chopping the onion, hacking through it without looking.)* Just like writin'. You should know, Ms Famous Published Psychologist. I read that book you wrote. Heck, it had even *me* cryin'— that death-bed scene with your Dad apologizin' and you forgivin' him? I thought they ruined it in the TV movie—I kinda saw *(A current Oscar-winning older actor)* in the part, not *(A current television star of questionable talent.)*

LIL: Yeah, me too. *(She throws a half-stick of butter into the skillet and proceeds to set the coffee table in front of the fireplace for dinner—place mats, silverware, napkins, candles.)*

ACT ONE

BLUE: Did you like my story? Did it hold your attention? I'm no Johnny Grisham, but I sure would like to give Stevie King a run for his money. You like him? Stevie King?

LIL: I really don't read him.

BLUE: You're kiddin'. Everybody reads Stevie King.

LIL: Not me.

BLUE: You're kiddin'! You know him, why don't you—

LIL: I've never laid eyes on him.

BLUE: You're kiddin'!!! You talk about him on the show all the time!

LIL: When?

BLUE: Just last week! Famous writer, certified genius, overcomin' incredible difficulties—

LIL: Hawking. Stephen Hawking.

BLUE: You don't know Stevie King?

LIL: No.

BLUE: Oh God. I'm sorry, I'm really stupid, I mean, it just shows you what a hick I am. *(Stabbing the knife repeatedly into the counter-top)* Oh god, god, god!

LIL: Blue, please, it's okay.

BLUE: No, it's not. I mean, here's me, never been around a celebrity in my life, I figure someone like you knows everybody.

LIL: I don't even know Stephen Hawking.

BLUE: I was gonna ask you to introduce me to him, help me get my stories published. Oh god. *(The onions:)* You want these in the skillet?

LIL: Yes, thank you.

BLUE: *(Dumping the onions into the skillet)* I do this a lot, you know. Assume things? Like for a while I thought *The X-Files* was all about me?

LIL: Would you mind cubing the veal?

BLUE: I just get so mad at myself for being so stupid.

LIL: Don't think about it. We all make mistakes.

BLUE: Yeah, but not like mine. And then I get careless.

(LIL *pushes parsley through the chopper as* BLUE *furiously cubes the meat.*)

BLUE: Like right now, I am so pissed at myself for being such a hick in front of you, I'll probably cut another finger off.

LIL: Careful, Blue. Be careful! Watch what you're doing with that—

(*Eyes on* BLUE, LIL *slices her own fingers in the machine. She screams, pulls out her hand.*)

BLUE: Goddammit, what did I tell you?!

LIL: Oh god!

BLUE: Serves you right, rushin' like that.

LIL: There's supposed to be safeties on these things!

BLUE: You don't believe that bullshit, do you?! Don't bleed on the counter! Hey, watch the food!!!

LIL: Take it easy!

(*This stops* BLUE, *making him feel even worse.* LIL *heads for the bathroom.*)

BLUE: I lost the tip of my finger in a soup once. We had to throw the whole thing out.

(*As* LIL *disappears into the bathroom,* BLUE *covers his eyes with a hankie and quietly cries. She re-enters, carrying a Band-aid, sees his emotion.*)

LIL: What's wrong?

ACT ONE 43

BLUE: *(Embarrassed, covering up)* I'm sorry if I blew up at you there. I'm a real calm person most of the time. I've had a hard coupla days, and I guess I just lost it.

LIL: *(Reluctant to get involved)* You wanna talk about it?

BLUE: Naaah. Maybe later. *(He dumps the meat into the skillet.)*

LIL: Bill said you called me on the show once. Is that true?

BLUE: Yeah, I guess.

LIL: Was I helpful?

BLUE: Kind of.

LIL: Well, if there's anything you wanna talk about—

BLUE: You ever treat people you know?

LIL: Not if they're friends. I'd send them to someone else. Why?

BLUE: But if someone you knew was troubled, would you help him? If you could give him the help he needs?

LIL: Sure. Is something wrong?

(BLUE approaches. As he talks, he gestures with the knife carelessly.)

BLUE: Yeah, well, I brought Owen here a coupla weeks ago and he was goofin' around and all of a sudden, well, part of what happened was cause I got mad— he was bleedin' and some of his blood dropped on the bearskin, and it's just a coupla drops, but man, I started screamin', "Don't bleed on Smokey!" I couldn't believe I was shoutin' like that. I got no control over my temper!

LIL: Let's put down the knife.

BLUE: *(Giving her the knife)* Oh. Yeah.

LIL: How'd he cut himself?

BLUE: Who?

LIL: Owen. You said he was bleeding.

BLUE: Oh yeah, he cut his thumb carvin' a whale out of a potato. He's like a little kid, see. His daddy don't take good care of him, so—I don't drink, and all the guys I know around here go out drinkin' every night and Owen can't drink either, and so—we hang out together. I watch out for him. We talk.

LIL: *(Starting her kitchen clean-up)* Sounds like you're a good influence.

BLUE: I try. I think he likes you, too.

LIL: *(Smiling)* He tried to steal my socks.

BLUE: Really?

LIL: Just yesterday.

BLUE: Don't worry, I'll speak to him.

LIL: Oh, he didn't mean any harm.

BLUE: He never does. He poured a whole bottleful of dishwashing liquid in the Jacuzzi once cause he wanted to make bubbles. Which reminds me—I wrote this story about this alien bubble—

LIL: Okay, Blue, if you want to give me a coupla your stories I'll look them over.

BLUE: Really? Aw, man! That's swell! I'll drop off a box of 'em after I take you into town. Maybe you could read 'em tonight. After your dinner, I mean.

LIL: We'll see.

BLUE: They're pretty scary, I'm warnin' you.

LIL: Takes a lot to scare me.

BLUE: Hey, why don't this guy you're meetin' tonight drive here?

LIL: What do you mean?

BLUE: It'd save time, you could get started on my stories sooner. I mean, instead of makin' me drive you twenty miles into town—

LIL: We're having a drink.

BLUE: You got drinks here. It's none of my beeswax, I know, but I was just—

LIL: The truth is, I've never met him, and I just wanted to check him out before I (brought him back—)

BLUE: Heck, I could check him out for you. Maybe I know the guy.

LIL: *(None of his business)* Blue, he's not— *(Deciding it's easier to explain)* He's from Tennessee. He's here for the cop convention in Plattsburgh. Here—look— *(Showing him the newspaper)* John Lone Wolf. He's the Hero of Chattanooga. He's won all kinds of medals. And he just did me a huge favor.

BLUE: What do you mean?

LIL: This idiot kept calling me—some house-sitter in Pittsburgh—and this guy got the Pennsylvania State Troopers to pay him a visit.

BLUE: Wow.

LIL: I called the convention center and everyone I spoke to said John Lone Wolf was an amazing guy.

BLUE: Still, it's good you're checkin' him out. There's lots of amazing guys out there who are lonely and horny and desperate. Present company excepted. You want me to stick around, have a drink with you?

LIL: No, it's not—

BLUE: I could drive you home if you don't like him.

LIL: If I don't like him, I'll take a taxi back.

BLUE: *(Laughing, only half-joking)* And have me for dinner instead?

LIL: *(Smiling, ultra-tolerant)* We'll see. You wanna do me one last favor?

BLUE: Sure.

LIL: Bring in some wood from outside. I want to have a fire when we get back.

BLUE: Sure. *(He heads to the pantry.)*

LIL: Or I get back. Where you going?

BLUE: Gettin' the wood. *(He disappears into the pantry.)*

LIL: There's none in there. I looked.

BLUE: *(O S)* There's a little door in the back. Opens right onto the wood pile.

LIL: I'll be in the bathroom, Blue! I'm gonna change! *(She moves toward the bathroom, singing to the tune of "Chattanooga Choo-Choo.")*

LIL: "Pardon me, Roy, is that the cat who chewed your new shoes?"

(LIL remembers her clothes and detours to the kitchen window, where they hang, as the phone rings. She pauses to hear who it is. After BILL's message, country-western music is heard playing over the phone machine: Crazy. *Laughing, she picks up the phone.)*

LIL: I'm on my way, Red. *(No response)* Hello? Red? Is that you?

CALLER #2: The woman I want to kill is you.

(In a fury, LIL slams down the phone. Silence, then she reaches for the clothes, only to reveal OWEN, faced pressed against the window behind where the clothes were hanging. She screams, and he screams too, frightened as she is. BLUE enters with an armload of wood.)

LIL: Dammit, Owen, what are you doing out there?! Get in here.

ACT ONE

(Clothes in hand, LIL *enters the bathroom and slams the door, as* OWEN *enters, stamping off his boots.* BLUE *deposits the wood.)*

OWEN: Hey, Blue. Where you been?

BLUE: *(Angry, speaking quietly)* Didn't I tell you not to hang around today? Didn't I tell you I needed some time alone with the lady?

OWEN: I forgot.

BLUE: You didn't forget. What were you doin' out there? Watchin' us?

OWEN: I was just lookin' for you, Blue.

BLUE: How'd you get here?

OWEN: I walked.

BLUE: Where from? My house?

*(*OWEN *nods.)*

BLUE: It's freezin' out there.

OWEN: Startin' to snow too.

BLUE: Why'd you walk? You wanna sneak up on us?

OWEN: No, Blue.

BLUE: You think you're gonna find us doin' somethin'?

OWEN: No, Blue.

BLUE: *(A teasing smile)* You got a crush on the lady, don't you?

OWEN: *(Embarrassed laughter)* No, Blue.

BLUE: Then why'd you steal her things?

OWEN: I didn't steal—

(Before he can finish, BLUE *smacks him upside the head.* OWEN *begins to cry.)*

OWEN: I'm sorry. I'm sorry, Blue.

BLUE: Yeah, I'm sorry too.

OWEN: You know I don't care about her.

BLUE: You better not.

OWEN: I care about *you*, Blue.

(BLUE *holds out a handkerchief—*)

BLUE: Here. Blow your nose.

(*—and* OWEN *blows into it.*)

BLUE: That all you wore? That thin little jacket?

(OWEN *nods.*)

BLUE: You'll catch your death of cold dressin' like that and I'm not gonna nurse you. And you know your daddy won't. (*He pockets the hankie and gets his heavy parka.*) Here, put on my coat. I'll be okay in the van.

(BLUE *holds his coat as* OWEN *puts one arm in a sleeve, and as* BLUE *tries to help him with the other sleeve* OWEN *circles and laughs.*)

BLUE: Owen, come on, quit foolin'.

(BLUE *succeeds in getting the coat on* OWEN *and starts to zip it up.*)

OWEN: Can't I ride with you?

BLUE: No you can't ride with us. Now you go on back to my house. I'll meet you there when I come back from taking the lady into town. Okay?

OWEN: How 'bout I meet you here?

BLUE: Nothin' doin'. If you're not home when I get back you'll be in big trouble. Comprende?

OWEN: You won't—you won't do nothin' to her, will you, Blue?

BLUE: (*A teasing smile*) You jealous?

(OWEN *smiles, shakes his head "no".*)

ACT ONE

BLUE: You better not be. Cause you know what I'll do to *you* if I catch you around here again.

OWEN: *(A blushing smile)* I know.

BLUE: Now zip this up good and tight and get goin'.

(BLUE guides OWEN to the door.)

BLUE: I'll tell her you apologize for upsettin' her and maybe you'll see her in town sometime before she goes. Okay?

OWEN: Okay.

(In the bathroom, the water shuts off.)

BLUE: Go on now. Here she comes.

OWEN: I miss you, Blue.

BLUE: Yeah, yeah.

OWEN: Bye, Blue.

(As OWEN exits outside and leaves, BLUE smells his armpits, then races to the spice rack where he gets a bottle of almond extract and dabs it under his arms and on his face and neck. As he puts it away, LIL enters from the bathroom, dressed for the evening. She places the clothes she was wearing earlier beneath the stairs near the Jacuzzi. He goes to get her coat.)

BLUE: My don't you look pretty.

LIL: Thanks. Where's Owen?

BLUE: He apologizes. I sent him home.

LIL: What did he want?

BLUE: *(Helping her on with her coat)* Me. He forgot I was spendin' the day runnin' you around, and he got a little worried. We better get movin'. We'll be late.

LIL: Wait a minute. What's that smell?

BLUE: What smell?

LIL: Smells like almond extract. I didn't put that in the stew, did I?

BLUE: Could be the wood I brought in.

LIL: I hope not. I hate that smell. *(Taking the directions)* I better take these directions so I don't get lost coming back. Where's your coat?

BLUE: I gave it to Owen. He didn't dress warm enough. I'll be okay.

LIL: You're really good to him, aren't you, Blue?

BLUE: I try. I give him what he deserves.

(Turning out the lights, BLUE and LIL are out the door, which she locks behind them.)

BLUE: *(O S)* You don't need to do that. We never lock up here.

LIL: *(O S)* I'm a city mouse, Blue. Humor me.

(BLUE and LIL walk past the windows to the car. After a moment, his van can be heard starting up, and driving away. The pantry door slowly slides open, and OWEN enters, removing the parka, and heads excitedly toward the stairs. Seeing her clothes, he stops. He gingerly touches her camisole, then picks it up and smells it. He slowly unzips his trousers as the lights fade to black. Music)

Scene Five

(Nine o'clock that night. The stage is silent, dark. Nothing has changed since we last saw it, except that OWEN is no longer there, the pantry door is closed, and a bowl and spoon sit on the stove beside the stewpot. Outside, the snow falls thick and fast. The wind roars. The chimes tinkle eerily throughout the scene. After a moment, we hear the mudroom door open, followed by the sound of a key in the lock. The front door opens, and a cold, exhausted LIL enters.

ACT ONE 51

She stamps her feet, closes the door, turns on the Jacuzzi for a nice warm soak. The phone rings. After BILL's *message,* RED's *voice is heard:)*

RED: *(V O)* Lil? It's Red. You there?

(LIL *immediately picks up. As she speaks she gets out of her boots and puts on slippers.)*

LIL: Where were you?

RED: *(V O)* Where were you?

LIL: I was there. A little late, but only by a few minutes.

RED: *(V O)* At the Ox?

LIL: Yeah.

RED: *(V O)* Five o'clock?

LIL: I thought we said six.

RED: *(V O)* Five.

LIL: Damn.

RED: *(V O)* Hell, it's probably my fault.

LIL: No, I do this a lot. I'm always getting times mixed up.

RED: *(V O)* Sorry.

LIL: Don't apologize.

RED: *(V O)* I called you about five-fifteen but you didn't answer.

LIL: That was you?

RED: *(V O)* Yours truly. You were home?

LIL: Fixing dinner. How many times did you call?

RED: *(V O)* Twice. I figured you'd left, so I didn't leave a message.

LIL: Oh god.

RED: *(V O)* What's wrong?

LIL: I picked up later, I thought it was you, it was the Pittsburgh weirdo. You said the state troopers told him to stop.

RED: *(V O)* They did.

LIL: Well now he's angry. He's threatening me. I want him arrested.

RED: *(V O)* I'll take care of it, don't worry. Boy, something sure don't want us getting together.

(Taking off her coat, LIL goes to the stewpot.)

LIL: How about tomorrow?

RED: *(V O)* Goin' home tomorrow. How about tonight?

LIL: You'd have to walk.

RED: *(V O)* What do you mean?

LIL: The snow's falling pretty thick. My taxi wouldn't come all the way down the road. I had to hike the last mile-and-a-half in the storm.

RED: *(V O)* Aw, Lil, I'm sorry.

LIL: Wasn't your fault. I'm the one who got the time wrong. On top of that this guy who gave me a ride into town made a pass at me.

RED: *(V O)* You're kidding.

LIL: Well, it wasn't much of a pass. He sort of stretched his arm across the back of the seat and put his finger in my ear.

(RED laughs. LIL does too.)

LIL: I didn't know it was him at first—I thought it was a bug. He's a sweet guy, he's just a little—needy. And then I get to the Ox and the bartender starts telling me his prostate problems. My life would be a hell of lot easier if I quit listening to everybody. *(Tasting the stew)* This stew is delicious if I do say so myself. You missed a good meal, Red.

ACT ONE 53

RED: *(V O)* What time did you get there?

LIL: The Ox? About six-ten.

RED: *(V O)* Aw, man—I left just a little before six—we must have passed each other on the road.

LIL: Really?

RED: *(V O)* Yeah. I got directions from the prostate bartender and I'm sure we drove right past each other.

LIL: Directions? Where to?

RED: *(V O)* Your place.

(A beat)

LIL: You came here?

RED: *(V O)* Yeah. Got there about six-thirty or so. The road was still okay then.

LIL: I'm sorry I wasn't around to let you in.

RED: *(V O)* Oh, that's okay. There was this little door open on the side by the woodpile? I got in that way.

(A beat)

LIL: You came inside?

RED: *(V O)* I didn't think you'd mind. I was cold. I thought I'd wait for you.

LIL: Why didn't you?

RED: *(V O)* Well, that's the thing—I came in and I—I wasn't the only one waiting.

(A breathless beat)

LIL: What do you mean?

RED: *(V O)* Some guy was there. Thick glasses, kinda slow—

LIL: Owen?

RED: *(V O)* He didn't give me his name. He was sorta—startled to see me.

LIL: What was he doing?

RED: *(V O)* Jerking off.

LIL: Oh God.

RED: *(V O)* He had a top of yours.

LIL: *(Noticing her camisole)* Oh my God. That's disgusting. *(She picks up the camisole and quickly takes it into the bathroom.)*

RED: *(V O)* Musta come in through the same door I did. Don't worry. He won't bother you again.

LIL: What did you say to him? Did you kick him out?

RED: *(V O)* In a manner of speaking.

LIL: What do you mean?

RED: *(V O)* Well, first I had a long talk with him. And then— *(Chuckling)* —you won't believe this—

LIL: What?

RED: *(V O. Chuckling)* —I don't believe it myself—

LIL: What? What happened?

RED: *(V O. Chuckling)* —it's just the funniest thing—

LIL: What did you do?

RED: *(V O)* I killed him. *(A beat. He laughs.)*

LIL: That's not funny, Red.

RED: *(V O. Laughing)* I know. I wanted it to be, but all that blood kinda dried up the laughs.

LIL: That's enough, Red. Now seriously, what did you do?

RED: *(V O. Sobering)* I'm sorry, I'm sorry. Seriously? Well, I seriously told him to take off his clothes and get in the Jacuzzi and then I took off my clothes—he thought I was gonna fuck him or something—and then I seriously got the butcher knife—you know, the one

ACT ONE 51

by the sink? And then I got in the Jacuzzi with him and I slit open his stomach.

(LIL *slams down the phone. She catches her breath, then looks to the Jacuzzi, slowly crosses to it, turns it off. Silence. Summoning courage, she looks under the soft plastic cover floating on top of the water. She reels in horror, her heart in her throat, letting the cover drop back into place. The phone rings.* BILL *gives his spiel. After the beep, through the answering machine we hear:)*

RED: *(V O)* Now you know why they call me Red. *(A beat)* I hope you didn't look in there. Not a pretty sight—a hot tub full of intestines. *(A beat)* What's going on here, you're asking. Who is this guy? Well, I'll give you a little hint. *(Dropping his Tennessee dialect, speaking precisely, evenly:)* I'm not John Lone Wolf from Chattanooga, Tennessee. Hold on a second, let me play something for you. You like surprises? Everybody likes surprises.

(A tape recorder button is pushed. CALLER #2 *is heard speaking.)*

CALLER #2: Hi, Lil. It's Daemon. Remember me? I need your help. I want your help. Only *you* can give me the help I need.

RED: *(V O. Laughing)* That was my little joke on you. Pre-recorded, just press the button. I hacked it through some number in Plattsburgh. Plattsburgh, Lil, not Pittsburgh. Ah, but don't worry, Daemon won't hurt you. Hell, I just made him up, he doesn't even exist. *(A beat)* But I do, Lily-pad. I'm your Last Resort. You ready for surprise number two? *(A beat. He sobers.)* I'm still here.

(LIL *stiffens, a terrified animal. Grabbing her boots, she heads toward the front door.)*

RED: *(V O)* I'm waiting right outside the front door.

(Alarmed, LIL backs away.)

RED: *(V O)* Or maybe I'm lurking in—what did Owen call it? The deer blind.

(LIL looks to the loft, uncertain.)

RED: *(V O)* Could be in the bathroom, the mud-room, anywhere.

(She crosses to the phone machine, drops her boots, disconnects RED, picks up the receiver, and quickly punches in 911. An Operator answers.)

911 OPERATOR: Nine-one-one.

LIL: I'd like to report an intruder. He's armed and dangerous, he—

RED: *(V O. Morphing from the 9-1-1 OPERATOR's voice)* How do you know I'm armed? *(A beat. He laughs.)* I do wonderful things with phone lines.

(LIL hangs up, looks around, then crosses quickly to the butcher knife, lying on the island. She grabs the handle then pulls her hand away. Her hand is sticky with blood. She grabs a towel, wipes her hand, picks up the knife with the towel between its handle and her skin. She grabs her coat and throws it over her knife-arm, then grabs her boots and, eyeing the loft and the front door and the bathroom, she backs toward the pantry, reaching behind her with her free hand to open it. As she does, a figure in BLUE's hooded parka and a horror mask falls out of the pantry, against her. She screams. But it's only a "scarecrow" stuffed with clothes [or a some sort of mannequin]. She slaps it, pushes it back into the pantry, as the phone rings and BILL's message plays.)

LIL: Where are you?!!!

(As RED speaks through the answering machine, she dons her coat and boots.)

RED: *(V O)* I wouldn't try to leave if I were you. People die of exposure out there in this weather. I'd just sit

ACT ONE

back, relax, wait for the storm to pass. If you're hungry, have some supper. That's what I did.

(LIL *looks to the stewpot.*)

RED: *(V O)* You know, you're an excellent chef, Lilypad. Your stew was mighty tasty. But it was missing a few ingredients. Parsnips—I love parsnips. And rutabaga—you like rutabaga? But even if you'd added parsnips and rutabaga, tomatoes, turnip greens, it still woulda lacked body. Your stew needed body. Owen agreed.

(LIL *gags, wiping her mouth as she circles the island, ending center-stage.*)

RED: *(V O)* Would you like to hear what he had to say on the matter? I made a recording of him too.

(*The click of a tape recorder button—*OWEN's *blood-curdling screams are heard, reverberating, as she sinks to the floor, fighting her fear, and we snap to black. Ella Fitzgerald sings "Let It Snow" as the house lights rise.*)

END OF ACT ONE

ACT TWO

Scene Six

(As the lights rise, we see Lil *just as we've left her. Outside, the wind howls, the chimes tinkle. After several moments of stillness, she slowly rises, knife at the ready. On the edge of hysteria, she desperately tries to calm herself and think clearly. She looks to the loft, then flips on the light, illuminating it. It seems to be empty. She cautiously climbs the stairs, and checks the space above. Just then, the phone rings.* Bill's *message begins to play, but stops abruptly in the middle, followed by a series of coded beeps. Puzzled about this, she heads down the stairs, bolts the front door, and moves into the pantry, where we hear her bolting the wood door. She strides back into the room, closes the pantry door, and bolts it shut also. She puts down the knife, opens the freezer, pulls out the bottle of Stoli, drinks from it, then gets a glass, pours herself another drink. A figure, unseen by her, passes by the kitchen window. She drinks from her glass, wandering down stage. Someone enters the mudroom, stamping snow off his feet. Panicked, she puts her glass on the coffee table and grabs the knife, then drops to the floor. A knock.)*

Egan: *(O S)* Hello?

(Silence. Lil's *frozen with fear.)*

Egan: *(O S)* Open up, please, it's the police.

(Should Lil *believe him?)*

EGAN: *(O S)* Are you all right in there? Hello!

LIL: What are you doing here?

EGAN: *(O S)* The guy who owns this place called the station. Asked someone to come and check on you. *(Silence)* Ma'am? Are you all right?

LIL: Let's see your i.d.

EGAN: *(O S)* Open the door.

LIL: Slip it under.

EGAN: *(O S)* Lady, I'm cold.

(Silence. LIL looks out the window, trying to see the car she didn't hear, as an identification card is slipped under the door. She grabs it, examines it closely.)

LIL: Where's your car?

EGAN: *(O S)* Down the road.

LIL: Why didn't you drive all the way?

EGAN: *(O S)* I got stuck.

LIL: How do I know that?

EGAN: *(O S)* Look outside, Lady. No one's driving in this weather.

LIL: Who's the head of the U S Federal Circuit Court for this jurisdiction?

EGAN: *(O S)* What?

LIL: It's the same judge up here as we have in New York City. If you're a policeman you should know his name.

EGAN: *(O S)* I don't believe this shit.

LIL: Do you want to come in or don't you? What's his name?

EGAN: *(O S)* It's a she. Marjorie R McNamera. And she's an asshole.

ACT TWO 61

(LIL *thinks a moment. Then she unlocks the door, and backs up with the knife.* DETECTIVE NICK EGAN *stamps in— middle-aged, not unattractive. He's covered with snow and freezing, wearing a winter coat, winter gloves. He shuts the door behind him, then spots the knife in her hand.*)

EGAN: Hi.

LIL: Where's your uniform?

EGAN: I'm a detective. I don't have one. What's with the knife?

LIL: Where's your suit?

EGAN: What?

LIL: Detectives wear suits.

EGAN: Not when the wind chill is twenty-five below. Please put down the knife.

LIL: What are you doing out here in a blizzard at nine o'clock at night?

EGAN: Jesus, what have you been cooking? Smells like a pigsty *(in here.)*

LIL: Why did you wait til the roads were impassable before you *(drove out here to…)*

EGAN: I'm doing my Christian duty as a fuckin' cop! *(Trying to calm down)* I just got back from a nice vacation to DisneyWorld, I'm out at the Placid Bar at the end of a long day, my wife who is never horny is waiting at home ready and willing, when your husband calls here—he can't get through, he calls again, he can't get through, he calls the station, they call me, I hop in the car, slide all over the highway, halfway down your little excuse for a road I get stuck in a snowdrift— *(Holding up a key ring with a tiny flashlight attached)* —I walk twenty minutes with this little dick for a flashlight, I'll never make love again because my balls are now solid ice, and I arrive on my mission of mercy to be given the third degree by some paranoid weekender with a really big butcher knife so would you put it the fuck down?

LIL: What's the name of the man—my husband—who called (in to the station?)

(EGAN *undoes his coat, revealing a flannel shirt and a shoulder holster.*)

EGAN: Oh my God, lady, I got a gun. If I wasn't a cop, if I was the homicidal snowman you seem to think I am, you'd be Swiss cheese by now. Could I have my I D? Please?

(EGAN *holds out a hand.* LIL *hesitates, lowers the knife, then tosses the I D to him. He puts it in his pants pocket, along with the keys and tiny flashlight.*)

EGAN: Thank you. Now what's your problem?

(*A beat.* LIL *nods to the Jacuzzi.* EGAN *looks toward it, then stares at her.*)

EGAN: Your Jacuzzi? You got a problem with your Jacuzzi?

LIL: Look inside.

EGAN: You're on the cliff-edge of hysteria because your Jacuzzi is on the fritz?

LIL: Look inside.

(*A beat.* EGAN *walks over to the Jacuzzi, lifts the plastic covering—*)

EGAN: I'm not a plumber, lady, I'm just…

(—*observes the carnage [which we, of course, don't see], and after a moment re-covers it. Silence*)

LIL: He's not all in there.

EGAN: How can you tell?

LIL: Some of him's in the stew.

ACT TWO 63

(EGAN *glances over at the stew pot. He says nothing for a moment, then excuses himself—*)

EGAN: Would you excuse me a moment?

(*—and heads to the bathroom, shutting the door behind him. After a moment, we hear* EGAN *coughing, the splash of liquid in water, then the flush of the toilet. Meanwhile,* LIL *sits on the couch and removes her coat. He exits the bathroom, shutting the door after him. He nods to the Stoli on the countertop.*)

EGAN: Mind if I have some of that? The Stoli not the stew.

LIL: Be my guest.

(EGAN *gets a glass from a cupboard. He doesn't even look for it, he knows right where it is. He pours himself a stiff shot—he's still wearing gloves—and drinks it.*)

EGAN: There's a myth going around that detectives get used to these things. Do you know who it is?

LIL: Owen. I don't know his last name. He lives with Blue down the road. I don't know his last name either.

EGAN: Owen Richards. You found him like this?

LIL: I went out about five-fifteen, came back about nine. It happened while I was gone.

EGAN: *(Pointing to her clothes on the Jacuzzi)* Whose clothes are those?

LIL: They're mine.

EGAN: Where's his?

(LIL *stares blankly at* EGAN.)

EGAN: I just saw—excuse this rather crude image—but I just saw a penis floating in among what appear to be intestines. Now unless he walked here naked, his clothes have to be around here someplace. Right?

LIL: Maybe…whoever killed him…took them away.

(EGAN *looks around, sniffs the air once or twice—*)

LIL: Or...maybe they're at the bottom of the Jacuzzi. Why does it matter?

(*—then wanders over to the trash basket and lifts the top to reveal* OWEN's *clothes, folded inside.* EGAN *carefully lifts them out.*)

LIL: How did you know they were there?

EGAN: I'm a detective. (*Examining them*) They're very neatly folded. Why would you mess him up like that and then neatly (fold his clothes?)

LIL: What do you mean "you"? You think I did this?

EGAN: The general "you". Just speculation. (*Placing them on the island*) Why are you still here? After you found him, why didn't you leave?

LIL: I was scared. I didn't know what I was going to do. Then you showed up and...

EGAN: Why didn't you call the police?

LIL: I tried. He wouldn't let me.

EGAN: He who?

LIL: He stops outgoing calls. I don't (know how.)

EGAN: Who wouldn't let you?

LIL: The man who did this.

EGAN: You know this guy?

LIL: Yes. No, I talked to him over the phone...

EGAN: You called him?

LIL: *He* called *me*. I don't know who he is but he wouldn't let me call out, he controls the phone lines.

(EGAN *studies* LIL, *then picks up the living room phone from where she dropped it in the last act and dials a number. She picks up the kitchen phone and listens. After a moment, his recorded voice answers, followed by his wife's.*)

ACT TWO

EGAN: *(V O)* Hello. This is Nick...

MRS EGAN: *(V O)* ...and this is Nancy.

EGAN: *(V O)* We can't come to the phone right now...

MRS EGAN: *(V O)* ...so please leave a message after you hear the little tone.

(We hear a beep, and the on-stage EGAN *says into the phone:)*

EGAN: Hi. It's me. You there? *(A touch of anger:)* Hello? *(He waits a beat then hangs up.)* Seems okay now.

*(*LIL *hangs up too, puzzled.)*

EGAN: Don't I know you?

LIL: What?

EGAN: How do I know you? You don't *look* familiar.

LIL: You ever listen to talk-radio?

(A beat. EGAN *realizes, laughs with pleasure.)*

EGAN: Oh God. Oh my God. Wait'll my wife hears about this. She listens to you every night.

LIL: Really?

EGAN: Every single night.

LIL: No wonder she's never horny.

EGAN: Jill, right?

LIL: Lil.

EGAN: Lil, Doctor Lil, yeah, right. Oh my god. *(Removing a glove, extending his hand)* Nicholas Egan. Pleased to meet you.

*(*LIL *reaches to shake hands, and realizes she still holds the knife.* EGAN *and* LIL *both laugh as she shifts the knife to her left hand in order to shake his. He grabs her right hand, twists it behind her, at the same time grabbing the knife*

from her left with his own gloved left hand. She cries out in astonishment and pain. He releases her.)

EGAN: Okay, Lil, let's get down to business.

(From a kitchen drawer, EGAN pulls a large freezer bag. He doesn't need to look for it—he knows where it is. He bags the knife, seals it, drops it in his coat pocket, takes off the coat and hangs it on a coat rack near the front door. He wears a sweatshirt jacket and flannel shirt underneath. He removes his remaining glove, then takes a pair of blue nitrile gloves out of his pocket and puts them on. All the while, he speaks:)

EGAN: What are you doing here?

LIL: Vacation.

EGAN: Alone?

LIL: My husband was supposed to fly in yesterday but something came up.

EGAN: You're tellin' me. How did Owen...

LIL: Shouldn't you call for help?

EGAN: I did. How did Owen...

LIL: When?

EGAN: When I got stuck in the snow. How did Owen...

LIL: Why aren't they here?

EGAN: *(Impatient, exploding)* There's a blizzard out there! What's the hurry?! The damage is done, you're safe, I'm here, they'll have to get a fuckin' snowplow to make it up the road, then they'll have to call in the guys from Albany to handle this mess, those idiots'll be two days draining that thing making sure they get all his pieces out of the little blowholes, so in the meantime why don't you tell me how did Owen end up inside the cabin, naked, and in your Jacuzzi?

LIL: Let's get something straight—I did not do this.

ACT TWO

EGAN: I didn't say you did. Did I say you did? I'm just asking questions, you seem to be avoiding giving me answers. What's that coming through the window?

LIL: I'm not avoiding (anything!)

EGAN: Case in point. What is that cable coming through the window? *(He crosses to it.)*

LIL: I'm doing the show from here next week.

EGAN: I thought you were on vacation.

LIL: Not according to my producer.

EGAN: Is it live?

LIL: Nine o'clock, five nights a week.

EGAN: No, I mean this cable.

LIL: It's hooked up to the utility pole outside.

EGAN: You by-passed the fuse box?

LIL: I guess so—yes.

EGAN: No wonder you're avoiding my questions. I'm gonna have to report this.

LIL: What?

EGAN: This is an illegal connection.

LIL: Oh, for God's sake, there's a tubful of intestines behind me and you're gonna cite me for cheating the electric company?!

(EGAN says nothing—just smiles.)

LIL: What do you want?

EGAN: His name.

LIL: Whose name?

EGAN: The name of the guy who did this.

LIL: He calls himself Red.

EGAN: *(Continuing his perusal)* Who is he?

LIL: I don't know.

EGAN: What's he look like?

LIL: To me he's just a voice. And some kind of telephonic Cassandra. Somehow he knew my husband wasn't gonna show. Somehow he knew I was gonna be snowed in.

EGAN: Maybe he checked the weather. *(Looking up to the loft)* You been upstairs since this happened?

LIL: Just to make sure he wasn't there.

(EGAN unsnaps his holster, takes out his gun, and climbs the steps.)

EGAN: How'd you meet him?

LIL: I told you I haven't. He called Friday night during the show. He made himself out to be a sort of psychotic killer.

EGAN: *(Looking down into the Jacuzzi)* "Sort of?"

LIL: Your wife didn't mention it?

EGAN: Mention what?

LIL: The last caller on the show. You said she listens every night.

EGAN: Oh, I'm sorry. We were with Goofy in Florida.

LIL: The station traced the call. They do that if someone's really on the edge, like a suicide, and won't give their number.

EGAN: What did they find?

LIL: He routed it through some number whose owners were away. In Florida.

(A beat. EGAN and LIL look at each other.)

EGAN: There were a lot of us down there last week. Did he call again? *(He re-holsters the gun, starts down from the loft.)*

ACT TWO

LIL: I thought you said she was home.

EGAN: Who?

LIL: Your wife. She didn't pick up when you phoned just now. You said she was waiting at home.

EGAN: Yeah. I thought she *was*. Did he call again? The guy who phoned the show.

LIL: He phoned here yesterday. Once as the psycho—he called himself Daemon—and several times as a policeman named Red.

EGAN: He said he was a cop?

LIL: Yeah.

EGAN: What did he want?

LIL: He was looking for his girlfriend, he…we had a friendly conversation. He called back this morning. I was to meet him in town at six, he (didn't show…)

EGAN: You made a date with a psycho?

LIL: The psycho is a character he made up, he's just—

EGAN: Oh, you hear that, Owen? You're safe.

LIL: He's a recording Red played over the phone. He said it was just a joke. He said—

EGAN: A laugh riot. Why would he do that?

LIL: I don't know, just to…freak me out. Or to get me trusting Red. I don't know why.

(*As* EGAN *heads to the island*)

LIL: He played another recording too.

EGAN: What was that?

LIL: Owen.

EGAN: (*Smelling* OWEN's *clothes*) He made a recording of Owen?

LIL: Yes.

EGAN: What did Owen say?

LIL: Nothing. He just screamed.

(A beat. EGAN's stomach isn't too happy to hear this, especially when he's standing right next to the stew pot and holding OWEN's clothes. He puts down the clothes.)

EGAN: Mind if I have another shot of, uh...

(LIL absent-mindedly motions to the bottle. EGAN pours himself a stiff drink. She moves to the coffee table—)

EGAN: Can I freshen yours?

LIL: No thanks. I don't...drink. I mean, I had one but... No thanks.

EGAN: Suit yourself.

(—and starts gathering the place settings and surreptitiously picking up her vodka glass. EGAN's back to LIL, he requests:)

EGAN: Please leave that alone.

(Without missing a beat LIL puts it all back.)

EGAN: What was Owen doing here?

LIL: I don't know.

EGAN: How'd he get in?

LIL: There's a door in the back room.

EGAN: And Red came here thinking he'd find what—you?

LIL: He knew I was out.

EGAN: Did he know Owen was gonna be here?

LIL: I don't think so.

EGAN: Why did he kill Owen instead of you?

LIL: I don't know. You don't believe me, do you?

(EGAN starts exploring around the TV.)

ACT TWO

EGAN: I'm just asking questions, Lil.

LIL: I'm sure you'll find his fingerprints all over the place.

(EGAN *pushes a button on the D V D player—*)

EGAN: How do you know he wasn't wearing gloves?

LIL: I don't know, maybe he was, but he was probably careless in some way. They always are, aren't they?

(*—and the D V D pops out.* EGAN *reads the title.*)

EGAN: *Sperms of Endearment.* One of my favorites.

(*He tosses the C D aside then moves to an ashtray with the half-smoked cigar and a piece of paper with some phone numbers.*)

EGAN: Whose cigar?

LIL: Mine.

EGAN: What's this number?

LIL: My husband's number in D C. In case someone needs to reach him. He rents this place out once in a while.

EGAN: And the number below it? It says "Jane". Who's Jane?

LIL: His secretary. Ex-secretary. He fired her last month but no one's been here to cross out that number.

EGAN: Why'd he fire her?

(*A beat*)

LIL: That's none of your business.

(EGAN *stops what he's doing and looks at* LIL. *Then, drink in hand, he exits into the pantry, unbolting the door as he does so.*)

LIL: I bolted that shut—and the door to the wood pile. In case Red decided to pay another visit.

(LIL *quickly moves to pick up her liquor glass again. She rinses it out in the sink, and dries it. She opens the cupboard and puts it away. Suddenly, something puzzles her. She looks to the cupboard, then to the drawer which held the plastic bags.* EGAN *re-enters, turning off the light in the pantry but leaving the door open. His glass is empty. He fills it again—he's getting a bit tipsy. She smiles and asks with seeming innocence:)*

LIL: How'd you know where the glasses were?

EGAN: What?

LIL: You went right to the right cupboard to get a glass.

EGAN: It was a hunch. I'm a detective.

LIL: What about the plastic bag—how'd you know where it was kept? And the bathroom—you went right to it.

EGAN: *(Chuckling)* I've been here before. *(He crosses to her clothes on the Jacuzzi.)* Why did you undress downstairs?

LIL: I was changing for the date. When were you here?

EGAN: You undressed beside the Jacuzzi?

LIL: I changed in the bathroom. When were you here?

EGAN: Last spring. I went fishing with your husband and a bunch of guys from town. We had dinner back here. I probably did the dishes, cleaned up. I always get stuck with that job.

(Smiling, LIL *heads for her coat on the couch.)*

LIL: How well do you know Jake?

EGAN: Not well at all. I only met him the once.

*(*EGAN *stops, looks at* LIL *as she takes the coat.)*

EGAN: That's not his name, is it? Jake?

LIL: No.

ACT TWO

(LIL *heads for the door.* EGAN *blocks her exit—*)

EGAN: What is this—a test? Are you testing me? (*—and tears the coat out of her hands.*)

EGAN: Siddown.

(EGAN *backs* LIL *into the ottoman.*)

EGAN: Sit. Down.

(LIL *sits.* EGAN *hangs her coat on the coat rack. He's become quite the belligerent drunk.*)

EGAN: See, I understand people like you. Always asking the questions. I tell the wife I was working late, processing some A and B at the station, the next thing she asks is, "Then what was your car doing at the Downtown Bar at one in the morning?" Where's *your* car?

LIL: I don't drive.

EGAN: I never met anybody up here who doesn't drive.

LIL: You ought to come to Manhattan then. It's a whole subculture there.

EGAN: See what I mean? What I just did to you—asking about your car—that's what she does to me. A simple question can completely change the subject. The thing is, I always forget to ask her, what was *she* doing out at one in the morning. And don't say she was out looking for me cause I know better. Fucking bitch. I'm a detective, see, and questions, questions aren't always about getting answers—sometimes they're meant to misdirect. Like what you were asking me just now. "How did you know where the glasses were?" You didn't care about the answer. You were trying to steer me away from *this*. (*From inside his sweatshirt pocket he pulls out her camisole.*) I found this stuffed in the waste basket in the bathroom. Looks like a perfectly good— top. Why were you throwing it away?

LIL: Something got spilled on it.

EGAN: *You're* telling *me. (He smiles, touches his nose.)* Bloodhound's nose. It's a gift. *(Sniffing the blouse)* I can smell baby shit locked inside a safe at a hundred paces. I can smell fear in the armpit of a shirt folded in a trashcan. But this ain't fear. And it sure ain't baby shit.

(A beat)

LIL: Owen broke in after I'd left. He took it from—my suitcase. He—masturbated and that's why I threw it away.

(EGAN *inhales the smell of the blouse again.)*

EGAN: He didn't take it from your suitcase. You were wearing this, weren't you, Lil?

LIL: No.

EGAN: *(Shoving it in her face)* But I can smell you on it too.

LIL: *(Moving away)* I wasn't wearing it when he—

EGAN: You mean you took it off before he came?

LIL: Stop making it sound like something it wasn't! I changed clothes, I hung it on the bathroom door or someplace, I was in a hurry.

EGAN: For what?

LIL: My date with Red.

EGAN: Are you sure it wasn't a date with Owen?

*(*LIL *sighs, frustrated beyond belief.)*

EGAN: Come on, Lil, I understand. He's lonely—

LIL: Look—

EGAN: —he found you attractive—

LIL: I wasn't trying to hide anything by (throwing it away—)

ACT TWO

EGAN: Did he rape you?

LIL: No.

EGAN: Did he have sex with you?

LIL: Of course not.

EGAN: Did you kill him?

LIL: No!

EGAN: Did you kill him?

LIL: No!

EGAN: Did you kill him?

LIL: No!!!

EGAN: *(Exploding)* Bullshit! You lie to me, you throw away evidence—

LIL: That is not why I— EGAN: —you make up a phone call from some cop named Red—

LIL: I did not make that up!

EGAN: Who else heard him?! Anybody?! Anybody see him?! He didn't show up in town, right?! You got an address on him?! A last name?!

(A beat—and then LIL *realizes:)*

LIL: I have his voice. *(Heading to the answering machine)* I hung up on him, he called back, he spoke to me through the answering machine.

*(*LIL *presses the play-back button on the answering machine. An electronic voice announces:)*

ELECTRONIC VOICE: No messages.

(Puzzled, LIL *presses the button again.)*

ELECTRONIC VOICE: No messages.

(Confused, LIL *tries to make sense of this.)*

LIL: That's crazy. He must have— *(She's at a loss, then remembers, in a panic.)* Wait a minute. The phone rang again. Right before you got here. He must have called in to erase his voice. He knew you were coming here. He somehow knew the code he needed to erase his voice!

EGAN: You know what? I am totally convinced. *(Silence. He returns to the kitchen to bag the camisole.)* But what about this Daemon's voice, the psychotic caller who isn't real.

LIL: Of course he's real, he just wasn't—

EGAN: You said Daemon didn't exist.

LIL: I said it was Red calling, disguising his voice.

EGAN: But how do I know Red's real?

LIL: Oh, for God's sake—

EGAN: The way I see it—

LIL: Don't you ever listen?!

EGAN: —you're drinking, you're watching dirty movies—

LIL: Get out of here!

EGAN: —you're horny, you're alone—

LIL: If you don't leave here (this instant—)

EGAN: —Owen shows up.

LIL: Get out!!!

EGAN: You give him a drink from your glass—

LIL: I did not start drinking until after I found him!

EGAN: Then why'd you wash it?

LIL: What?

EGAN: When I was in the pantry just now you washed the glass and put it away. Why?

LIL: It was dirty.

EGAN: Yeah, with Owen's fingerprints.

LIL: Oh dear God—

EGAN: Why'd you wash it, Lil?!

LIL: I didn't want it in the police report! *(A breath, then:)* I stopped drinking three years ago—and so should you! I'm a role model for some people. If the internet got hold of this—

EGAN: I see what you mean: "Sloshed Shrink Butchers Boyfriend".

LIL: *(Heading for a window)* Where are they?

EGAN: Sit down!

LIL: They should be here by now.

EGAN: Who?!

LIL: Your buddies! Why aren't they here?!

EGAN: They'll be here!

LIL: *(Grabbing her coat at the door)* I'll meet them on the road!

EGAN: *(Drawing his gun)* You can't even see the road so sit the fuck down!

(LIL *stops.*)

EGAN: Put down the coat.

(LIL *does.*)

EGAN: That's a good girl.

LIL: I just—

EGAN: Shut up and sit down.

(LIL *sits on the couch.*)

EGAN: It's an open-and-shut case, far as I can see. You're sitting here alone, missing your husband, watching some D V Ds you got for a hot romantic weekend that isn't gonna happen cause of the storm. Owen's standing at the window, watching you, you turn him on, he pushes his way inside, holds a knife to your throat, unbuttons your blouse, and jacks off. *(Moving toward her, to sit)* Or maybe you fuck him. Something goes wrong—he's too aggressive, not aggressive enough—I don't know, you're the shrink, you figure it out. But that's when you go for the knife. Is that how you hurt your finger, Lil? Did you cut yourself when you grabbed the butcher knife?

(EGAN touches LIL's bandaged finger, then puts his arm across the couch behind her. After a moment she leans back against his arm.)

LIL: Whatever you say.

EGAN: Whatever I say? Aren't you cooperative?

(LIL puts her hand on his knee.)

LIL: Would you like some coffee?

EGAN: No thanks.

LIL: I'm going to make some coffee.

EGAN: I don't need coffee.

LIL: *(Rising, heading for the kitchen)* I do.

EGAN: *(Following her)* I'm keen as a bloodhound, sharp as the wood-saw you must have used to cut him up. What were you gonna do with the pieces, Lil? Feed 'em to your wayward husband? That's why he fired Jane, right? I remember him talking about her last spring, about him fucking his secretary. He was worried you'd find out. And you did and he fired her—but you're still pissed, aren't you?

(As the scene continues, LIL fills the coffee-maker with water and grounds, turns it on, then gets a cup from the cupboard. EGAN pours himself another drink.)

LIL: Yeah. Probably.

ACT TWO 79

EGAN: "Yeah. Probably." You're just like my wife. She'll play along just like you're doing now, and then all of a sudden the lady ain't home when she's supposed to be home. You want my opinion? I think she's fucking one of the guys she teaches with— *(Laughing)* Listen to me. What the fuck is it with you? Why do people keep telling you their personal problems?

LIL: I'm a good listener.

EGAN: "I'm a good listener." My wife talks about you all the fucking time. You're such a generous person with advice on the radio, but in real life? *(Gesturing with the gun)* You're just a basket full of bullshit like the rest of us.

LIL: *(Pushing the gun away)* Would you please be careful (where you point that?)

(EGAN *grabs* LIL's *wrist, twisting it behind her back.)*

EGAN: Hey, hey! What the hell are you up to?!

LIL: I'm just (trying to get the gun out of my face!)

EGAN: I'm not stupid! I'm not one of your brain-dead fans! *(He puts down the gun, takes his handcuffs and places one end around her wrist—)* I got experience too! I dealt with psychos too! Not over the phone, face-to-fuckin' face!

(—then fastens the other end to the oven door handle. LIL *grabs for* EGAN's *gun but he gets it first, then removes any potential weapons out of her reach, and pours another drink. She tries to pull loose but can't. He re-holsters the gun.)*

EGAN: But you thought you could put one over on me, right? The dumb fuck cop from Lake Placid? Guess again, Lil. N Y P D, fifteen fuckin' years. I saw more horror down there than even *God* could think up. And someone like you comes along who believes these fuckers can be fixed and lo and behold you're as fucked up as any of 'em. I do not need shrinks like you telling me I don't have the stomach for this job! *(Moving to the Jacuzzi)* It was my goddamn wife who fell apart. She put in for the transfer, picked a name she liked. "Lake Placid." *(Lifting the cover and looking in)* Such a nice name. Such a nice town. She said we wouldn't find shit like this in Lake—

(EGAN drops the cover, fights sickness, then heads to the bathroom, slams the door. We can hear him gagging behind the door. LIL immediately grabs the kitchen phone and dials the Operator.)

OPERATOR #1: *(V O)* Operator.

LIL: Gimme the police. Lake Placid police.

(The call rings through. A male voice answers:)

DESK SERGEANT: *(V O)* Lake Placid Police.

LIL: You sent a Detective Egan out to Fishkill Road, he's abusive, he's drunk—

DESK SERGEANT: *(V O)* Detective Egan?

LIL: Yes. He says he called in for help but no one's arrived yet.

DESK SERGEANT: *(V O)* You must be mistaken, ma'am. Detective Egan was killed three months ago in the line of duty. Could you hold please?

(He puts her on hold. Inside the bathroom, EGAN is silent. Noticing the plastic-bagged knife sticking out of his jacket, LIL puts down the receiver without hanging up and tries to reach for it. No go. Quick-thinking, she grabs a pair of tongs from a kitchen drawer and stretches as far as she can. She manages to pull the bag out of his coat with the tongs. She hides it in the oven, then, as the toilet flushes, quickly hangs up the phone just as he re-enters from the bathroom.)

EGAN: Who you calling?

ACT TWO

LIL: Blue. I thought he might be able to get your car out.

EGAN: What'd he say?

LIL: He's not home.

(EGAN *picks up the phone—*)

EGAN: Let's visit our friend Mister Redial.

(*—and presses the redial button. The phone rings, and we hear a different Operator:*)

OPERATOR #2: *(V O)* Operator.

EGAN: Cut the bullshit, Lil. *(Hanging up the phone, taking out the handcuffs key)* You want the key to the handcuffs? It's right here. Nice and handy. *(Putting the key into his shirt pocket)* Just gimme a confession. Tell me how you killed him.

LIL: It was like you said. It was just like you said.

EGAN: Okay. Now we're getting somewhere. Was it an accident?

LIL: He attacked me. I killed him in self-defense.

EGAN: *(Crossing to the bottle, pouring another drink)* Then why'd you cut him up? There's some holes in your story, Lil. I know—maybe we should re-enact this. I'll be Owen. You're watching the dirty movie and he comes up behind you, rubs against you, slips his hand under your blouse—

(LIL *turns to pour coffee into a cup.* EGAN *takes a drink, his back to us, and tucks his shirt in.*)

LIL: Maybe we should start with coffee? I made enough for two. I brought these beans all the way from New York City. Special blend. I mean, with a nose like yours, if you like coffee at all, you'll want some of this!

(LIL *throws the hot coffee into* EGAN's *face. He screams, covers his eyes.*)

EGAN: You bitch!

(LIL *grabs the knife from inside the oven just as* EGAN *runs to grab her, thrusting the knife—still in the plastic bag—into his stomach. He stops, backs off. Silence. He looks down at the handle, sticking out from him, then moves away. He doesn't understand what's happening. He collapses onto his knees, and then onto his back, right of the island, near the open pantry door. He continues to breathe, very much alive. She watches this all in shocked silence. Outside the wind is howling. Then she moves quickly, trying to keep panic at bay. She tries to undo the handcuffs, notices the screws on the oven door handle and starts pulling open drawers.)*

LIL: Screwdriver. Where's a fucking screwdriver?

(LIL *finds a screwdriver, which she uses to frantically unscrew the handle on the oven door. All the while,* EGAN *slowly, with difficulty, reaches for his gun. With a surge of strength, she rips one end of the handle away from the oven door and slips the cuff off the handle. She picks up the nearest phone to dial 9-1-1. The wind's roar heightens. The call rings through.)*

LIL: Answer, please answer.

(*Suddenly, just as* EGAN'S *hand grasps his gun, all the lights flicker and go out. The phone, because it is electrically powered, dies. Dim blue moonlight outlines the kitchen window. He, however, is thrown into utter darkness.)*

LIL: Oh God.

(LIL *heads to a bureau where she finds a powerful lantern flashlight. She turns it on, aims it at* EGAN. *He holds his gun, aiming it vaguely at the flashlight. She quickly puts down the flashlight as he fires the gun, missing her, breaking some glasses in a cupboard. Meanwhile, in the darkness, she circles carefully around the island behind him. Hearing her, he turns and fires the gun again. She grabs the gun, they struggle, but in his weakened stake he can't fight and she*

ACT TWO

manages to pull it away from him. She kicks him, he cries out, she strikes him with the butt of the gun, knocking him senseless. Then, gun in hand, she retrieves the flashlight, checks to see he is out cold. She picks up the kitchen phone again—it's dead.)

LIL: Oh god. Fuck. No power. Where's the rotary?

(She points the light to the loft and the rotary phone. She climbs the steps to the loft. At the top she takes the phone, dials 911. It rings, and the Operator answers.)

9-1-1 OPERATOR: 9-1-1.

LIL: *(A mile a minute)* There's a man here impersonating a cop, he's already killed someone, he attacked me, there's a power outage, I can't see—

9-1-1 OPERATOR: Slow down, ma'am. Where are you?

LIL: Fishkill Road, somewhere down—

9-1-1 OPERATOR: Where on Fishkill Road?

LIL: I don't know, you gotta turn and—

9-1-1 OPERATOR: Do you have an address?

LIL: It's a P O box.

9-1-1 OPERATOR: How about directions? Can you give me directions?

LIL: Oh God—wait—there's a map—don't go away.

(Leaving the phone, carrying the gun and flashlight, LIL *fearfully, carefully, climbs down the stairs and goes to the side table where she last saw the directions. They aren't there. She sweeps the room desperately, looking for the map, but stops, gasping, when her flashlight strays to where* EGAN *collapsed. He is no longer there.)*

LIL: Oh my God.

(The sound of breaking wood splits the silence, as if someone were prying open the back door in the pantry, trying to get out, or in. Gun in hand, LIL *heads to the pantry door,*

pausing to rest the flashlight on the island so that its beam faces upstage, away from the door. She moves through the dark toward the door, slides it closed and bolts it shut. Relieved, she backs along the upstage side of the island, still aiming the gun, then turns, pausing just left of the flashlight beam to catch her breath. She sighs, relieved. Silence. Suddenly, EGAN *leaps, roaring, out from behind the cooking island just behind her, into the beam of the light, grabbing her. She screams, pushes him away, backs away from him quickly in the dark. He moves toward her, zombie-like, and she fires the gun in the air to warn him.)*

LIL: Stay away from me! Stay away!

(But EGAN *doesn't stop.* LIL *aims and hits him in the shoulder with the next shot. He falls back against the island, still standing, swaying, trying to keep his balance, like a wounded monster. Then he takes another step toward her. She fires again, this time at his legs. He flies back against the island and slips to the floor. He tries to rise. She fires again, but the gun is empty. She throws it down, climbs in a panic to the loft and picks up the rotary phone.)*

LIL: Hello? Are you there? *(No answer. She's sobbing, near hysteria.)* Hello? Is anyone there? *(No answer. What can she do? She shouts into the phone:)* Help! Help me! Oh dear God, won't somebody help me?!

(A beat. Then over the phone we hear:)

RED: *(V O)* I'd like to, Lil.

(In horror, LIL *drops the receiver. She rushes down from the loft and gets the flashlight, then shines the light on the pantry door—it appears to be locked. She runs to it to make sure—yes, it is locked. She shines the light on the front door—it's not locked. Panicked, she races to the front door to lock it, then drags a bench and the ottoman in front of the door to block it. She returns to the living room to drag something else upstage too, but she stops, sensing that she's not alone. She shines the light on the pantry door—it's till*

ACT TWO

locked. She shines the light on EGAN's *body, then on the living room door, then across the Jacuzzi to the bathroom door. Nothing. Slowly she lets the light climb the loft stairs rung by rung, and swings it slowly from stage left to right until the beam lands on someone crouched in the loft, watching her. He is dressed in a dark hooded parka and ski mask which covers his entire face, and carries a shoulder pack. Slowly he removes the parka hood, the ski mask. It is* OWEN.)

LIL: Owen?

(RED *turns on a high-beam flashlight that he carries, shining it on her face.*)

RED: Red. Owen's gone. Owen isn't around here anymore. *(Heading for the stairs)* I tried to get in the back way but you bolted it shut. I had to use the ladder from Blue's van to get in up here. *(As he descends the stairs, he removes his thick glasses and speaks in the* DESK SERGEANT's *voice:)* Lake Placid Police. Detective Egan was killed three months ago. Could you hold please? *(jumping the last few steps to the floor)* Funny thing is, he really *was* a cop.

(RED *starts whistling "Chattanooga Choo-Choo", placing his flashlight near the Jacuzzi as* LIL *makes a dash for the front door, trying to move the furniture out of the way. He calmly moves to her, turning her around, taking her flashlight from her and pushing her downstage as he speaks in his Tennessee dialect:*)

RED: Look at it this way, Lil: I'm younger, I'm stronger, I'm smarter—

(RED *puts* LIL's *flashlight down and brings her arms behind her, clicking the dangling cuff around her free wrist so that her hands are now handcuffed behind her back. All the while she is fighting hysteria, trying to stay in control. A losing battle.*)

RED: —don't even try.

(RED *pushes* LIL *gently onto the couch, pulls a third high-beam flashlight from his shoulder bag, then heads for the stewpot.*)

RED: Poor Owen. He didn't know what to make of me at all. I was just some voice he kept hearing, whispering all these nasty thoughts from the dark. And listening. I love to listen. You and I have a lot in common, Doc. (*He ladles stew into the bowl on the counter.*) Mmmmm—love that almond extract. Blue always did make a terrific stew. (*Offering her some*) Blue Plate Special?

(LIL *turns away in disgust.* RED *laughs, taking a bite.*)

RED: Relax, it's mostly veal. Blue's in the hot tub. I figured you wouldn't want to poke around til you found a *head*. One man's intestines looks pretty much like everyone else's. (*He drops the bowl in the sink.*)

LIL: How did you do this?

RED: It was easy. Blue taught Owen the basics—phone systems, computers—but neither of them had the inventiveness I brought to it. Like running the phones through a laptop in the butcher shed out back. Then sending you calls that were pre-recorded, just like that telemarketing bullshit you get all the time. Calling in a bomb threat to keep your husband from getting here. Who thinks of shit like that? Then this cop walks right out of the storm into your mudroom and I thought it was all over. The one thing I didn't plan for. I didn't count on you handling him better than I could. (*Laughing, he takes a digital recorder out of a pocket.*) I want you to hear something.

(*He pushes a button and it plays a recorded phone conversation. As it plays,* RED *removes his coat and shoulder*

ACT TWO

bag, then moves back to the kitchen to pour himself a cup of coffee.)

LIL: *(V O. Recorded)* Hi. Welcome to Last Resort.

BLUE: *(V O. Recorded)* Doctor Lil?

LIL: *(V O. Recorded)* You're on the air.

RED: Soon as he heard you were coming up here for a visit, Blue gave you a call.

BLUE: *(V O. Recorded)* I got this friend, Doctor Lil. And he has this problem.

RED: He'd met you just the once, but he saw that as permission to get some free advice.

LIL: *(V O. Recorded)* Okay. And what's your friend's problem?

BLUE: *(V O. Recorded)* It's like one time he's one person and then another time he's someone else. He's got these very different personalities.

LIL: *(V O. Recorded)* You mean—you think he's a multiple?

BLUE: *(V O. Recorded)* I don't know. But sometimes he's this smart-alecky genius—

RED: *(Sitting on the living room steps near* EGAN*)* I like that—"genius."

BLUE: *(V O. Recorded)* —and sometimes he's this really sweet kid.

LIL: *(V O. Recorded)* Well, first you need to understand—if he is a multiple, that probably stems from childhood trauma, most likely sexual.

RED: Stupid.

LIL: *(V O. Recorded)* And the remarkable thing about multiples is that the differences can be physical as well as psychological. The various personalities may have different eyeglass prescriptions—their brain waves can even change from one manifestation to another.

(Leaving his coffee cup on the floor in front of EGAN, RED *hops onto the couch beside* LIL.*)*

RED: Psycho-babble. Blah-blah-blah.

LIL: *(V O. Recorded)* Nevertheless, none of those personalities is a fully formed individual.

LIL: *(V O. Recorded)* If you're concerned about your friend, you should take him to a qualified therapist who can integrate (the different personalities…)

BLUE: *(V O. Recorded)* Like you?

LIL: *(V O. Recorded)* I'm really not able to (diagnose this over the phone…)

RED: Here it comes.

BLUE: *(V O. Recorded)* But if someone like you were to work with this kid in person, you think you could cure him?

LIL: *(V O. Recorded)* Possibly, yes, but—

(RED *turns off the recording and tosses the digital recorder onto the couch.)*

RED: Cure him? Cure him?! You're talking about ending my life!

LIL: I did not agree to—

RED: You just said it! You may call it integration, but I call it murder. And I call this self-defense.

LIL: I'm not an expert on curing multiples—

RED: So you'll send me to someone who is. Analysis, then medication, then integration and I am gone.

LIL: You won't lose who you are. You'll just become part of a more fully-formed (individual…)

ACT TWO   89

RED: Bullshit! I am not some splinter of a shattered ego! I did this so you could see what a well-rounded, fully-formed individual I am! *(Calming, gently touching her face)* Once you see that, we can be friends. Of course, I'll still have to slit your throat.

(RED heads to the kitchen sink to get a glass of water—out of sight of EGAN—and as he does so, she sees EGAN moving, his hand clawing for a gun that isn't there—he's alive, and conscious. LIL thinks fast.)

LIL: Blue didn't say a word about you, Red. He talked about alien pods and carnivorous underwear. He thought I was the key to getting his stories published. You understand me? He thought I was *the key*.

RED: Shut up.

(Taking his cue from LIL, EGAN lifts his hand to his shirt pocket where he put the handcuff key. Pulling out the key—which sparkles in the darkness—EGAN weakly holds it out, and LIL moves into position so he can pass her the key, but before she can get it, RED spots her, though he still does not see EGAN on the floor.)

RED: Whoa, whoa, whoa—get away from the door.

(Reluctantly, LIL moves downstage, away from EGAN and the key. RED drinks the water. LIL glances at the coffee cup near EGAN.)

LIL: I almost got away. For a second I thought—my cup runneth over. My cup runneth over.

RED: You're not making sense, Lily-pad.

(Taking her cue, EGAN reaches, with agonizing slowness, to place the key into the coffee cup. It drops with a soft clink. EGAN groans with the effort. Hearing the groan, RED finally spots him.)

RED: Well, what do you know? Annie Oakley missed. *(Crossing to EGAN)* God, Lil. You left him to bleed to death? I thought you were kinder than that. *(Standing over* EGAN*)* Oh, man, look at you. These women, I tell you—you handcuff them to a stove, they don't like it.

*(*RED *kicks the knife handle;* EGAN *groans in pain.)*

LIL: Stop that!

RED: Oh, now you feel sorry for him. Do you know any First Aid? *(Putting down the flashlight, removing his belt, re-looping it)* The Boy Scout Handbook says, in case of severe bleeding, you have to apply a tourniquet. Question is, where do you tie it? Oh, wait, I know. We'll put it here.

*(*RED *whips the belt over* EGAN*'s head and pulls it tight around his neck, jerking* EGAN *to his knees.* EGAN *chokes. She screams:)*

LIL: Oh God!!! Don't. Please don't.

RED: You think I enjoy this? It's never pleasant.	LIL: I'll do anything, anything you want.
RED: I know you will, Lil. That's beside the point.	LIL: Don't! Please don't do this! Don't!!!

*(*LIL *rushes at* RED*, kicking him.* RED *pushes her away and jerks the belt even tighter.* EGAN *struggles for air.)*

RED: Why do you care about him?! You should thank me, Lil! You wanted this, didn't you?!

LIL: No!

*(*RED *slams* EGAN*'s head against the island to quiet him, then drags him behind the island. Only his legs can be seen—kicking, writhing.)*

RED: Then why'd you shoot him? Stab him? Whatever the hell you did! Yee-haw!!! *(He stoops to pull the knife out of* EGAN*.)*

LIL: Red, please, let him live.

ACT TWO

RED: Man, you shoved this in good. You're an animal, Lily-pad. (*Pulling out the knife, he removes it from the plastic bag, wipes it clean of blood.*)

LIL: I'll help you any way I can.

RED: God, what a mess.

LIL: Just let him live.

RED: But you did this, Lil. We're a lot alike, you know. I'm just finishing what you began.

(RED *suddenly thrusts the knife [out of sight] back into* EGAN's *body. Again. And again.* EGAN *stops kicking.* LIL *sobs. After a moment,* RED *rises, catching his breath.*)

RED: Not fun. Not fun.

(RED *tosses the knife onto the counter behind him.* LIL *moves toward the coffee cup.*)

RED: Whew! Work like that sure makes a cowboy thirsty. (*He grabs the flashlight, then crosses to pick up the cup of coffee with the key in it.*)

LIL: No.

RED: No what?

(LIL *pauses, fractionally.*)

LIL: We're not alike.

RED: Wanna bet?

LIL: What I did was in self-defense.

RED: Me too. Only I knocked him out first, so I'm a little more compassionate than you. (*He starts to sip the coffee, then stops, and looks at it. He looks up at her, then down at the coffee again. Has he seen the key?*) Got milk? Don't bother. (*A mockery of* OWEN) "I'll do it. I'm here to help."

(RED *puts the flashlight on the island and opens the refrigerator. The light inside, of course, is out. He finds a carton of milk. He puts down the cup, opens the milk.* LIL *notices the coil of cable and the black box. Her mind races.)*

LIL: Red? Did you cut the power?

RED: Who else?

LIL: I thought it was the storm.

RED: Guess again. One little snip, Lily-pad, the line to your fuse box is history.

LIL: You cut the line to the fuse box?

RED: Yep. And now I'm going to cut *you*. *(He finishes adding milk, takes a sip of coffee, then picks up the knife.)* You pride yourself on compassion and forgiveness and being oh-so-civilized? Well, there's a part of you nobody's ever seen, and I'm going to slice you open til I find it. *(He slowly approaches for the kill.)*

LIL: There's a part of you that doesn't want this to happen. Owen doesn't want this to happen.

RED: Bullshit.

LIL: And what about Daemon? What does he want?

RED: There is no Daemon. I made him up.

LIL: Why?

RED: I wanted to fuck with you.

LIL: You wanted my help.

RED: No I didn't.

LIL: You asked for my help.

RED: That was bullshit.

LIL: You wanted to warn me! Why else would you call my show? Whether it was Daemon or Owen—

(Grabbing the bottom of LIL*'s blouse,* RED *slices it open.)*

RED: There is no Daemon or Owen! There's only me!

LIL: Then prove it to me!

ACT TWO

(This stops RED.*)*

RED: How?

LIL: Let me help you.

RED: How? Twice a week on the couch? Forty-five minutes every Tuesday and Thursday? Oh, I forgot—you don't fix things over time, Lil. Five minutes and you're on to the next commercial.

LIL: Then give me five minutes.

(A beat)

RED: Like I'm one of your callers?

LIL: Only face-to-face. Five minutes with Doctor Lil.

(Smiling, RED *heads to the island.)*

RED: Okay, I'll play. This'll be fun.

*(*RED *puts down the knife, picks up a kitchen timer, sets it for five minutes and place it near the stewpot.)*

RED: Welcome to *The Last Last Resort*. Five minutes. Give me your best shot.

LIL: Owen?

RED: That's not my name.

LIL: I know. I want to talk to Owen.

RED: He's gone, Lil.

LIL: I don't think so. Owen?

RED: I told you. He's dead.

LIL: Owen?

RED: Shut up.

LIL: Owen.

*(*LIL *speaks steadily, with unflappable calm.* RED *too is calm, though she seems to be getting to him.)*

LIL: I know you'e in there, Owen. I know you can come out if you want to.

RED: Shut up.

LIL: Come out, Owen.

RED: No.

LIL: You may think he's stronger but he's not. You were the first. You were the first-born.

RED: No.

LIL: You can do it, Owen. Come out. I need to talk to you.

OWEN: I'll—do—it—

(RED *stumbles to the floor, between* LIL *and the coffee cup.*)

RED: No!

(RED *gasps, the struggle over. He looks up. Who's won? Silence, then:*)

OWEN: I did it. *(Dawning joy)* Didn't I?

LIL: *(Smiling)* Yes, Owen. You did. Good for you.

(LIL *moves toward the cup on the island.* OWEN *grabs her leg, stopping her, as he begins to cry.*)

OWEN: What if he comes back?

LIL: He won't. Not unless you let him.

(OWEN *pulls her down to sit on the stairs behind them.*)

OWEN: I can't stop him.

LIL: Yes you can.

OWEN: Help me.

(OWEN *collapses in sobs, putting his head in her lap, a needy child embracing a protecting parent.*)

LIL: You can do this. You're strong. You're so strong.

OWEN: I'm not.

ACT TWO

LIL: You told me once I should never underestimate you. You're right. I shouldn't. And I never will again.

(RED *smiles through, mischievous and devious:*)

RED: Bullshit. You just did. *(Laughing, caressing her)* You shrinks, you'll believe anything if it's what you want to hear. Like your husband saying he loves you. Like your Daddy saying he's sorry he molested you. I read your book, Lil! You sat at his deathbed while he apologized, believing every word he said, but I bet what he really wanted was to fuck you one more time.

LIL: *(Furious, losing it)* Like your Daddy fucked you?!

(A beat, then RED *pulls away, stands:)*

RED: I don't know what you're (talking about.)

LIL: How old were you when he started? Three? Four?

RED: He never laid a finger on me.

LIL: Was he drunk?

RED: You know nothing about my father.

LIL: I know he hurt Owen! I know whatever he did gave birth to you! You were born because some little boy was raped!

(Silence. The animal in LIL *now unleashed, she begins stalking* RED. *He backs away.)*

RED: You don't know what you're saying.

LIL: Oh yes I do.

RED: You're making this up.

LIL: We are a lot alike. Just like you said.

RED: This is just more of your (psycho-babble bullshit.)

LIL: I know what it's like to be six years old and feel his hand creep up your leg in the dark! I know what it's like to hear the same voice that sings you lullabies whispering how good you make Daddy feel! I sure as fuck know what it's like to be filled with a rage so awful you just want to him to die! You think I didn't feel that? You think I don't live with that every day?!

(RED *has stopped, clearly fighting something he doesn't want to hear.* LIL *circles him.*)

LIL: But I can talk about it. That's the difference between you and me. You can't say a fucking word. Go on! Say it! Tell me what it was like to smell his cheap aftershave and taste the liquor on his breath. Feel his weight on top of you! Say it!!! Tell me how you struggled when he covered your mouth so you couldn't scream.

(RED *screams, in agony, in fury, collapsing to the floor, puking with dry heaves.* LIL *heads for the island and the coffee cup. In silence, she takes the key from the cup. Then:*)

RED: *(Rising, determined)* You don't know shit.

LIL: I know enough to make you sick.

(RED *turns out two of the flashlights, circling for the kill.*)

LIL: I know about survival, Red. I survived my Daddy—and I'm sure as hell gonna survive you.

(*Taking the knife,* RED *slices open his T-shirt. The timer dings— Time's up.*)

RED: It's Jacuzzi time, Lil. Time to get wet.

(RED *turns out the final flashlight, the one on the island.* LIL *circles downstage of him. We see that her hands are now free of the handcuffs.*)

LIL: *(Pleading)* Red?

RED: What?

LIL: *(Dropping the plea, and the handcuffs)* You first.

(LIL's *hands free, she throws the handcuffs at* RED, *distracting him, then races to the stove. He runs to her, but before he can reach her she throws the contents of the stewpot*

ACT TWO

in his face. He screams, drops the knife. Stewpot in hand, she runs for the front door. He runs behind her, pulling her away, but she whacks him in the balls with the pot, then in the head, and throws the pot at him. He catches it with a grin and she turns to run up the stairs.)

RED: Run, Lil, run!!

(RED slowly moves up the stairs after LIL, enjoying every moment of the chase. She throws suitcases at him; he tosses them easily down the ladder.)

RED: I'll do it! No one ever allows me to do what I know I can do!!!

(As RED reaches the top of the stairs she grabs the can of air freshener and sprays him in the face. He screams, covers his eyes. She seizes the rotary phone and whacks him across the face with the phone, its bell dinging loudly. He loses his balance, and he swings around the outside of the loft railing, dangling now over the Jacuzzi. She lifts the phone and brings it down hard on his hands. Screaming, he releases his grip and falls onto the soft bubble-wrap cover [which supports no weight] and into the Jacuzzi. Water splashes high. In seconds she is down the ladder again, as he splutters to the surface.)

RED: Goddammit, Lil! You broke my fucking hand!

(She grabs the power cables coiling out of the box, flips the On switch, and heads in his direction as he struggles to get out of the Jacuzzi. He sees what's about to happen.)

RED: Hey, Doc, no, let's have some compassion here!

(LIL tosses the plug cables at RED with all her might—)

RED: NNNNNOOOOOOOO!!!

(—and as soon as they hit the water, the Jacuzzi, as well as the distribution box, explodes with light, sparks flying, smoke sizzling. RED jerks, screaming, with electric intensity, until he sinks under and dies. Silence. LIL stands—angry,

hurting, falling apart—then collapses onto the couch, accidentally turning the digital recorder on as she does so. Her voice is heard.)

LIL: *(V O. Recorded)* A lot of us have been hurt very badly by people we trusted, but violence—whether it's against ourselves or others—isn't the answer.

(LIL *begins to laugh at the ludicrousness of this advice.)*

LIL: *(V O. Recorded)* It may be entertaining but it's not going to solve our problems.

(Unseen by Lil, blinking red lights from an arriving police car light up the trees outside. Her laughter dies as she begins to realize the horror of what she's done, become, of what lies ahead, of what has been done to her.)

LIL: *(V O. Recorded)* We survive with reason, reserve, and compassion.

(As the lights fade to black:)

LIL: *(V O. Recorded)* Hi. Welcome to *Last Resort*. You're on the air.

END OF PLAY

CASTING NOTE

In addition to the onstage cast of five, you'll need one woman to do the voices of Caller #1, D V D Woman, Mrs. Egan, an Operator, and the 911 Operators, as well as one man to do the voice of Bill. These can be pre-recorded or done live, or a mixture of both.

Other actors double as the voices of Officer Parker and his partner, the Sound Man, the D V D Man, and an Operator, all pre-recorded. The actor playing Owen also does the voices of Caller #2 (Daemon, pre-recorded), Red (Live), and the Desk Sergeant (Pre-recorded).

PROGRAM NOTE

When listing the cast in the program, only the following should be named: Caller #1, Lil, Hack, Bill, Caller #2, Owen, Red, Blue, Egan. A question mark (?) should follow "Caller #2" in place of an actor's name, and a pseudonym and false pic and bio should be used for the actor listed as playing "Red" unless the theater knows an appropriate-looking actor who will allow his name and likeness to be used. If not, use this one:

LENNY BLACKBURN (Red) is pleased to make his (city) debut in this production. He has appeared in several of Mr Pielmeier's plays, and his favorite roles include Einstein in Arsenic and Old Lace, Adolphus in Major Barbara, Feste in Twelfth Night, and Kafka in Metamorphosis. (The first letters of these roles, oddly enough, are an anagram of his best-kept secret). He first played a character named Red in When You Comin' Back, Red Rider? at the Indiana Rep, where he also attended the Indy 500, his second passion. He is married to actress Leona Kay, and is the proud father of Kanada and Merrily.

PRODUCTION NOTES

Given the grisly nature of this piece, I suggest that it be performed without the use of any blood. Leave the violence to the audience's imagination.

The four major screams in the play are the Owen-at-the-window appearance in Scene Four, the hooded-parka/horror-mask scarecrow in Scene Five, the Egan leap in Act Two and the appearance of Red in Act Two. If done well, you'll hear both men and women shriek, but they must be carefully planned and worked out far in advance of tech.

Owen must not be seen or lit until the exact moment when Lil takes down the clothes.

The scarecrow should look real, like something right out of a horror movie.

In order for the Egan leap to be effective, the island (behind which he jumps at her) needs to be positioned roughly stage-right to stage-left, not at too-sharp an angle. A space needs to be built under the island for him to hide, so that when Lil passes by him after she bolts the pantry door, her hip can hug the edge of the island and it will appear to us as if no one could possibly be there. Also, the sound of the breaking wood should be quite startling—we must completely believe that he is in the pantry and nowhere else. Once she passes by him and sighs, the actor should wait two beats before jumping, just enough time to give the audience—and Lil—a false sense of security.

Red's appearance should take care of itself, as long as he is dressed head-to-toe in black, so that we don't see him at all until the light illuminates him, or possibly a few moments before Lil becomes aware of his presence. There needs to be some sort of trap door hidden in the loft for Red's entrance. He enters during the gun-shots, when our attention is diverted elsewhere.

The lights must be very selective—err on the side of less rather than more. Scene Three may be lit by the firelight, the T V light, her reading lamp, and the lightning. Scene Five should have areas of shadows (the kitchen) or total darkness (the loft). When the blackout happens in Act Two, there should initially be no light except that from Lil's flashlight; very little ambient light should be added until after Red's entrance. The three flashlights used in this last scene must be carefully choreographed to do much of the lighting of that scene. Obviously the lighting designer must help when needed—illuminating the coffee cup, the distribution box, some of the fight, etc—but always subtly and carefully. Avoid shining the flashlights into the audience.

There needs to be a sound-proof booth back-stage from which the live calls originate. This booth must be equipped with a video monitor. Red's and possibly Bill's calls should be live whenever possible.

Egan's gun when it first appears should be a dummy with no bullets. He switches for a gun with blanks when he enters the bathroom the second time. The knife in Egan's belly is really a half-knife attached to a steel plate that can slip down into his pants. It rests on top of the island, covered by a tea towel, during Act Two. When he takes his last drink and tucks in his shirt (with his back to the audience), he is really tucking the knife into place. If done simply and casually, no one will see it until we want them to see it.

And don't forget to heat the water in the Jacuzzi. Pity the poor actor.

www.ingramcontent.com/pod-product-compliance
Lightning Source LLC
Chambersburg PA
CBHW071724040426
42446CB00011B/2206